JENNINGS SOUNDS THE ALARM

Also by Anthony Buckeridge:

JENNINGS
SOUNDS THE ALARM

Seven plays for radio

by

Anthony Buckeridge

with illustrations by Val Biro

DS
David Schutte

Text copyright © Anthony Buckeridge 1948, 1949, 1999

Illustrations copyright © David Schutte 1999

First published in 1999

by DAVID SCHUTTE

119 Sussex Road, Petersfield, Hampshire GU31 4LB

Illustrations by Val Biro

ISBN 0 9521482 2 6

A CIP catalogue record for this book
is available from the British Library

Typesetting by KT

Printed in the U.K. by

Polestar AUP Aberdeen Limited

CONTENTS

ILLUSTRATIONS

INTRODUCTION

I had, for some while, been writing radio plays for BBC Drama department before *Jennings at School* arrived on the scene. I had never thought of becoming a children's author: indeed, the first Jennings play was planned as an observation on the adult reaction to the workings of the juvenile mind. Children say and do the most extraordinary things which to their way of thinking are logical, but to the grown-up mind seem bizarre and lacking in reason.

This was the germ of the idea, but it didn't work out like that. Soon the humour of the situation got the upper hand and set the scene for a play with a strong line of comedy, characterisation and plot.

The first Jennings play made its way from Drama department to Children's Hour in 1948. David Davis, the producer, liked the story-line and the characters and asked me to enlarge the first play from a one-off to a series of six: which I did.

Next year a second series was commissioned and this continued for sixteen years until the demise of Children's Hour, by which time I had written 62 scripts, all of which were repeated on air several times over the years. Children's Hour *Request Week* was a popular twice-yearly competition in which listeners voted for their favourite programmes. *Jennings at School* managed to head the list every time.

David Davis was a skilful producer and chose a talented cast. Geoffrey Wincott and Wilfred Babbage played Mr Carter and Mr Wilkins - well contrasted roles. The boys had to be changed every two or three years as their voices broke and they sounded too old for their parts. Several of them went on to become well-known in later years, most of them on the stage, though Glyn Dearman joined the BBC as a producer and Jeremy Clarkson, in later years, became a motoring journalist and TV presenter. When *Jennings at School* came back for four years in a series called Fourth Dimension (produced by Herbert Smith) Wilfred Babbage had retired and I took over the role of Mr Wilkins, a part I very much enjoyed.

The plays were normally scheduled for broadcasting in the late autumn or early spring. David would start rehearsals on the day before transmission and continue until shortly before it was time to go on the air. In the early days the performances were 'live', but in later years they were recorded for broadcast at a later date. During the era of live broadcasts there was, of course, the remote possibility that something could go wrong: a boy might fluff a line or turn over two pages of his script at once. I remember a crisis of this sort happening on one occasion and it was soon covered by some quick-witted *ad libbing* by Geoffrey Wincott who was at the microphone with the unfortunate offender. However, once the recording was safely in the can there was little to worry about and all concerned could relax.

I am grateful to David Schutte for suggesting that the plays should be published as a series of books and for undertaking the work of preparation. The scripts have not been updated or altered in any form: these are the plays as they were first written. I am also grateful that David has persuaded Val Biro to illustrate the cover and each of the plays in his inimitable style. Val Biro has recaptured the essence of the Jennings stories in a way which is both humorous and appealing.

So now, to complement the stories in book form, we can add the radio versions on which so many of the books were based. Read them, record them, or act them: Jennings, Darbishire and the rest await your attention.

Anthony Buckeridge
October 1999

JENNINGS
LEARNS THE ROPES

(First series no.1)

Jennings Learns the Ropes was the first Jennings play.

It was first broadcast by the BBC Home Service for Children's Hour
on 16th October 1948, with the following cast:

MR. CARTER	Geoffrey Wincott
JENNINGS	David Page
DARBISHIRE	Loris Somerville
TEMPLE	Derek Rock
VENABLES	John Bishop
ATKINSON	John Cavanah
BUS CONDUCTOR	Laidman Browne

Fade in

MR. CARTER: (*checking*) Ration book, clothing book, identity card, sweet coupons, health certificate. Right; what about bank?

ATKINSON: Fifteen shillings, sir; in this envelope, sir.

MR. CARTER: Fifteen shillings for Atkinson. Thank you; next boy.

JENNINGS: Me sir, please, sir.

MR. CARTER: A new boy, eh; and what's your name?

JENNINGS: Jennings, sir.

MR. CARTER: Oh yes, here you are on the list. J.C.T. Jennings; ten years, eight months; right?

JENNINGS: No sir, not quite, sir.

MR. CARTER: Oh?

JENNINGS: Eight months and three weeks, sir.

MR. CARTER: We won't worry about that. Have you been to a prep school before?

JENNINGS: Not a boarding school, no, sir.

MR. CARTER: Then we'll have to show you the ropes, shan't we? But first, I want your ration book, clothing book... yes, sweet coupons, they're with your ration book, I expect.

JENNINGS: Here they are, sir.

MR. CARTER: Yes. Identity card, yes. Any money for the bank?

JENNINGS: I've got a pound, sir.

MR. CARTER: Jennings... One pound. Health certificate?

JENNINGS: I don't think I've got one, sir.

MR. CARTER: You must have. How do we know that you're not suffering from mumps, measles, chicken-pox, whooping-cough, scarlet fever and bubonic plague?

JENNINGS: Oh, but I'm not, sir; I'm quite well really; I haven't got any spots, sir.

MR. CARTER: But if you haven't got a health certificate... what's that in your pocket?

JENNINGS: Is this it, sir?

MR. CARTER: It is; thank you. Now let's get someone to show you round. Venables!

VENABLES: Yes, sir?

MR. CARTER: Come and be introduced. On my left, Venables, easily distinguished by his trailing boot-laces.　●

VENABLES: Oh, sir!

MR.CARTER: On my right, Jennings, who's got to be looked after. Venables... Jennings: Jennings...Venables!

Bell sounds, distant

There's the tea bell. Take Jennings to the dining hall and treat him like you would your... no, I've seen how you treat your brother... look after him as you do yourself and he certainly won't starve.

VENABLES: Oh, sir!

Cut to quiet murmur of voices which ceases abruptly

MR. CARTER: Benedictus, benedicat.

Scraping of chairs followed by buzz of conversation.

Fade to background and hold under:

VENABLES: You'd better sit here, Jennings, next to this other new chap. Here you, what's your name?

DARBISHIRE: Charles Edwin Jeremy Darbishire.

VENABLES: You can keep the Charles Edwin Jeremy, you won't be needing it. You'd better talk to Jennings as you're both new.

DARBISHIRE: Oh, had I?   ...Magnificent weather for September, isn't it?

JENNINGS: Uh? Oh yes, super... I say, how much cash have you got in the school bank? I've got a pound.

DARBISHIRE: I did have a pound, but I spent fourpence halfpenny on the way here this afternoon, so I've got, er, - nineteen and, er, - I've got a pound less fourpence halfpenny. I gave it to that master who said grace just now; what's his name?

JENNINGS:I think he's Mr... er, I say, Venables, what's that master's name?

VENABLES: Benedick. We all call him that, anyway. Actually, he's Mr. Carter.

JENNINGS: Why call him something else, then?

VENABLES: Well, you heard him say grace just now. Benedictus and all that.   And after meals he says "benedicto, benedicata".

11

JENNINGS: So what?

VENABLES: Benedick Carter.

JENNINGS: Oh. Is that a joke?

VENABLES: You're a bit wet, aren't you?

DARBISHIRE: It's Latin, Jennings. My father knows a lot of Latin; he's a clergyman.

JENNINGS: Well what does all that benedict... whatever it is, mean?

VENABLES: Dunno. I was thirteenth in Latin last term; no good asking me. I'll ask Bod, he's a brain. (*Calling*) Bod, what does the grace mean in English?

TEMPLE: Well, when they say it before meals it means something like "come and get it", and after meals it means "you've had it".

JENNINGS: But if what Bod says is right...

VENABLES: You can't call him Bod, Jennings. New chaps aren't allowed to call fairly senior chaps by nicknames until their second term.

JENNINGS: Then his name isn't really Bod any more than Mr. Carter's name is Benedick?

VENABLES: 'Course not. His name's Temple, and his initials are C.A.T. so naturally we call him Dog; which becomes Dogsbody for short.

JENNINGS: But it isn't short, it's longer.

VENABLES: Okay then, it needs shortening. Bod short for Body and dogsbody short for dog. Really, you new chaps are dim at picking things up.

DARBISHIRE: My father says that the word nickname is derived from the Anglo-Saxon word eke-name and means...

TEMPLE: If you don't stop telling us the story of your life and pass me a hunk of bread you'll get an eke-name where you don't want it. Really, these new chaps! That's what Socialism's done for us.

ATKINSON: Pass the ozard, Jennings.

JENNINGS: The what...?

ATKINSON: Ozard.

JENNINGS: I don't know what... d'you mean the jam?

ATKINSON: What else could I mean?

JENNINGS: But why is it ozard?

ATKINSON: Because it's rotten muck. All school food's muck, but if it's nice, it's called wizard muck and the opposite of wizard is ozard; see?

JENNINGS: I think so.

ATKINSON: School jam stinks, so it's ozard. Everything that's ozard, stinks.

JENNINGS: I s'pose it does.

ATKINSON: Yes. You're ozard.

Cross fade background noise to conversation in dormitory

VENABLES: You sleep in this bed, Jennings; and you're next to him, here, Darbishire. Go on, you've only got ten minutes. Did you write your postcard home, after tea?

JENNINGS: Yes, I gave it to Mr. Bened... er, Mr. Carter.

VENABLES: What's the matter with you, Darbishire?

DARBISHIRE: (*gulping*) I don't like this place much. When I'm at home, my father always comes and talks to me when I'm in bed and... well, it's all so different here, isn't it, Jennings?

JENNINGS: I s'pose we'll get used to it in three or four years.

VENABLES: You'll have plenty to get used to; wait till you get into Old Wilkins' Latin class. That's right, isn't it, Atkinson?

ATKINSON: Yes, you don't know you're born till Wee Willie Wilkie gets to work on you.

TEMPLE: He made me write out the passive of Audio twenty-five times; it nearly killed me.

VENABLES: And if you stop when you're going through a verb, if you take a breath even, you get a stripe. I got fifty-seven stripes for Latin last term.

JENNINGS: Does he get very angry?

ATKINSON: We call it breezy. Does he get breezy? Sometimes there's such a super-duper breeze that the windows rattle. The thing to do is stand behind him so's you can watch the back of his neck turning red. It's wizard... if it's not you he's on about. You'll have a great time with Wilkie, Jennings; he's ozard.

JENNINGS: What are the others like?

TEMPLE: Mr. Mitchell's a bit of a crab; he doesn't shout like Wilkie, but the quieter he gets, the more of a bait he's in.

13

(*Mimicking*) Temple, come here; you miserable specimen, you crawling earthworm, is your insignificant brain unable to grasp the fact the angles at the base of an isosceles triangle are equal? Write it out a hundred and fifty million times before tea.

DARBISHIRE: I don't think I'm going to like this school.

JENNINGS: Are they all like that?

VENABLES: Benedick's all right. He's a bit crackers at times, but all masters are anyway; they have to be. When a school wants a new master, they go to the nearest loony bin and pick out the screwiest. Now, what else have you got to know? You mustn't put your hands in your pockets unless you're a prefect.

DARBISHIRE: Supposing I want my handkerchief?

VENABLES: Sniff or wait till you're made a prefect. You mustn't run in the corridors, you mustn't use fountain pens, you mustn't read comics, you mustn't eat tuck before lunch, you mustn't wear your vest for football, you mustn't wear your cap like a spiv and if you make a duck in a house match your name'll be mud for the rest of the term.

DARBISHIRE: But I always do make a duck; I'm no good at cricket.

TEMPLE: We'll start calling you mud now, then. That'll get you used to it.

Bell rings

ATKINSON: Gosh, that's the five minutes bell. Come on, let's get washed. Hurry up with that basin, Venables. And another thing, Jennings, you have to wash your feet every night unless it's your bath night.

Noise of gargling

VENABLES: I say, Atki, can you change gear when you're gargling. I can, listen.

Gargling and gear changing

JENNINGS: I can be a super jet fighter; listen. Eeee-ow-ow-eeee-ow-ow, dacka-dack-dack-dack-doyng.

ATKINSON: What's the doyng for?

JENNINGS: That's the other plane crashing when I've hit him.

ATKINSON: I can do it better than that. Eeee-ow-ow-eeeeow-ow...

All join in accompanied by gear-change gargling

OMNES: Eeee-ow-ooow; dacka-dacka-dacka-doyng! Eeee-oow-oow...

Noise stops abruptly

MR. CARTER: It would improve matters considerably if dormitory number four fighter squadron would make a forced landing and get back to base. In other words, this light is going out in three minutes and if anyone's not in bed, there'll be trouble.

OMNES: Yes, sir.

MR. CARTER: Where's Jennings?

JENNINGS: Here, sir.

MR. CARTER: Come here. The chief reason why I told you to write a postcard after tea was so that your parents could learn of your safe arrival, plus any other items that you thought might interest them.

JENNINGS: Yes, sir.

MR. CARTER: Did you read your card through when you'd written it?

JENNINGS: No, sir.

MR. CARTER: Then I'll read it to you. (*Reading*) Dear Mother I gave mine in to Mr. Cater Darbsher has spend four and a half d. of his my healthy certiket was in my poket he said I had got mumps or bubnic plag it was a joke we had wizard of oz at tea Atkion says oz stinks so do I. Temple is a bran he is short for dogsboody love John. (*Stops reading*) If your mother can understand what all that's in aid of she's a better man than I am, Gunga Din. You'd better write it again in the morning. I shall be back in ninety-five seconds to put this light out.

VENABLES: Hurry up, you chaps, get a move on. Carter means it when... here, Jennings, what are you doing at that basin.

JENNINGS: Washing. You said I'd got to wash my feet.

VENABLES: But you can't have that basin first; it's Bod's. New chaps have to wash last.

JENNINGS: Well, I'm here now.

TEMPLE: That's my basin, Jennings, get out. The cheek of some new chaps.

JENNINGS: Well, I didn't know.

15

TEMPLE: You ought to know; first wash always goes by seniority; it's a rule. Go on, get out of the way.

JENNINGS: I was here first; I'm going to wash first. I'm half-washed as it is.

TEMPLE: Are you going to get out of my basin?

JENNINGS: No, not till I've finished. I think it's a daft rule.

ATKINSON: I wouldn't stand that from a new chap, Bod.

TEMPLE: I'm not going to. If you don't get out, Jennings, I'll squeeze this wet sponge down the back of your pyjamas.

JENNINGS: My father said I'd got to stick up for myself when I went to boarding school. You can go and chase yourself.

TEMPLE: All right then.

Jennings lets out a piercing scream and bursts into tears

JENNINGS: You've soaked me. I'm all wringing wet!

ATKINSON: Cave, Carter!

MR. CARTER: Who was responsible for that screaming noise?

JENNINGS: (*still tearful*) Bod was, sir; Temple, sir. He squeezed a wet sponge down the back of my pyjama trousers and made me all wet.

OMNES: Sneak!

MR. CARTER: Jennings, you don't quite understand. I didn't say "who made that noise", I asked who was responsible for its being made. That gives the culprit the opportunity to own up without laying the victim open to the charge of telling tales. There's a difference, you see.

JENNINGS: Yes, sir.

MR. CARTER: If we all learn to own up, there'll be no need for tale-telling. In any case, I never listen to them… Perhaps I was deafened by that extraordinary noise you were making a moment ago and I didn't quite catch the answer to my question. Who was responsible for that noise?

TEMPLE: I was, sir.

MR. CARTER: Thank you, Temple. We'll go into the merits of the case in the morning. Come and see me after breakfast.

TEMPLE: Yes, sir.

MR. CARTER: By the way, Temple, your sweet coupons weren't in your ration book.

16

TEMPLE: My mother's posting them on to me today, sir. I'll give them to you tomorrow, sir.

MR. CARTER: All right. Silence now and lights out. Good night.

OMNES: Good night, sir.

Click of light switch and door shuts.

Slight pause

TEMPLE: You rotten sneak, Jennings; you wait. I'll bash you up tomorrow.

ATKINSON: Good old Bod; do it before tea, that's the best time.

JENNINGS: It wasn't my fault.

VENABLES: 'Course it was. You needn't have yelled your head off like that, you great baby.

ATKINSON: And why tell Benedick? He ticked you off for sneaking, anyway.

DARBISHIRE: My father says we must speak the truth in all circumstances, even if...

ATKINSON: Shut up, Darbishire. We don't want to hear what your father says.

DARBISHIRE: I was only going to say that my father insists that truth...

TEMPLE: Put a sock in it. Any more from you and I'll bash you up tomorrow when I've finished with Jennings. And you can tell your father so, with my love.

DARBISHIRE: Yes, Bod.

TEMPLE: My name's Temple and I don't let new chaps call me anything else.

Pause

ATKINSON: Jennings!

JENNINGS: What?

ATKINSON: Temple won the house boxing championship last year. Oh boy, what a bashing-up it's going to be. Rare, super-duper, wizzo and smash-on. I'll be in the front row.

JENNINGS: I don't care.

DARBISHIRE: I don't think it's fair when Jennings was only asserting his...

17

VENABLES: Shut up, Darbishire, nobody asked you. You know, Jennings, you're taking on a big job when you get on the wrong side of Bod.

ATKINSON: He doesn't give tuppence for anybody. D'you know what he did last term? He foxed into town during prep.

JENNINGS: What's that mean?

ATKINSON: Well, you're not allowed into town. And Bod forced his way out when Wilkie was taking prep and caught a bus into town and went to Valenti's.

DARBISHIRE: What's Valenti's?

ATKINSON: Never heard of Valenti's? No of course you wouldn't. It's a big sweet shop; they sell Brighton Rock. Anyway, Temple went to Valenti's, bought six-pennyworth of rock and brought it back in a bag with the shop's name on to prove he'd been. And he wasn't caught.

TEMPLE: That's the sort of chap I am. Of course, it's easy if you've got the nerve. Still, no one else has ever done it; there's no one except me who'd dare to. Well, good night, chaps... Oh, Atki, remind me to bash Jennings before tea. And Darbishire, too, if he starts getting uppish.

ATKINSON: Righto, Bod; good night.

Fade out; pause and fade in

JENNINGS: What's the matter, Darbishire? You haven't been crying, have you?

DARBISHIRE: No, not really. I've just been wishing I was at home and it's made my glasses go all misty.

JENNINGS: You've got nothing to worry about. How about me? I'm due for a bashing-up before tea.

DARBISHIRE: Well, so am I if I get uppish.

JENNINGS: Have you been getting uppish?

DARBISHIRE: No, I've been feeling downish all morning. I say, I don't like boarding-school, do you? I wish I was at home.

JENNINGS: That's silly; we only got here yesterday.

DARBISHIRE: But everything sounds so awful. You heard what they said in the dorm last night. About the master who goes red in the neck and the other one who makes you write things out a hundred and fifty million times. I was trying to work out in bed, last night, how long it would take to write

18

something out a hundred and fifty million times. I made it just over thirteen years, without stops.

JENNINGS: P'raps they were exaggerating.

DARBISHIRE: But there's other things. I'm no good at games and I'll probably get bashed up every time I let a goal through or make a duck or something. I wish I'd never come here.

JENNINGS: I wish my father was here, so's he could tell me what to do. He told me to stand up for myself, and I did over that wash-basin and now it's led to something worse.

DARBISHIRE: Oh dear, I'm so miserable. I never thought it would be like this. My father says we must always strive...

JENNINGS: I say, shall we run away?

DARBISHIRE: Run away?

JENNINGS: Go home. Then you can tell your father you don't like it here, and my father can tell me how to stand up for myself against the house boxing champion. He'd know a way... if there is one.

DARBISHIRE: But how can we go home? We're not allowed out.

JENNINGS: We could just walk out before tea and get a bus to the station and go home. We could ask Mr. Carter for our pounds out of the bank, then we can buy our tickets.

DARBISHIRE: But I've only got nineteen and something. D'you think that'll be enough to get to London on?

JENNINGS: 'Course it will. It'll be ever so exciting.

DARBISHIRE: But s'pose we get caught?

JENNINGS: P'raps we ought to disguise ourselves. We'd have more chance then.

DARBISHIRE: What, beards and false noses and things?

JENNINGS: Yes.

DARBISHIRE: But I haven't got a beard. I'd look silly wearing a beard with short trousers anyway.

JENNINGS: I could wear your glasses, that'd be something; and you could, er, - you could walk with a limp. Then they mightn't recognise us.

DARBISHIRE: (*cheering up*) Coo, yes, wizzo. Like this, look.

JENNINGS: No, bags I walk with the limp. I can do it rather well.

DARBISHIRE: That's not fair. You said I could have the limp. Besides, there's nothing else for me to have.

19

JENNINGS: Well, you won't be wearing your glasses.

DARBISHIRE: But it isn't a disguise just to be not wearing something.

JENNINGS: Well, you can carry a stick and turn your collar up.

DARBISHIRE: Yes and wear my sun hat with a dent in the top like a trilby.

JENNINGS: We must remember not to wear our school caps.

DARBISHIRE: I say, Jennings, couldn't we both walk with a limp?

Fade to:

MR. CARTER: So you both want some money from the bank, do you?

JENNINGS: Yes please, sir.

MR. CARTER: How much?

JENNINGS: A pound, please, sir.

MR. CARTER: That's rather a lot, isn't it? What d'you want it for? (*Pause*) Well, don't you know?

JENNINGS: Do we have to say what it's for, sir?

MR. CARTER: A large sum of money like that on the second morning of term's a little unusual. I can't let you have it unless you tell me why you want it.

JENNINGS: Oh... Yes sir; it's all right then, sir; don't bother, sir.

DARBISHIRE: How much could we have without having to tell you what it's for, sir?

MR. CARTER: I wouldn't be curious up to about sixpence.

DARBISHIRE: Is that all, sir?

MR. CARTER: I'm afraid so.

JENNINGS: Then may we have sixpence, please, sir?

MR. CARTER: All right; here you are... Er, – Jennings!

JENNINGS: Yes sir?

MR. CARTER: Don't spend it on anything foolish, will you?

Fade to:

DARBISHIRE: Well, I s'pose that's that, Jennings. And I was feeling quite excited about walking with a limp with my collar turned up. I was going to try and look like Edward G. Robinson.

JENNINGS: What, in short trousers and school socks?

DARBISHIRE: Well, not really like him, but that sort of chap. Still, it's all a washout now.

JENNINGS: No it isn't. We've got enough to get to the station on the bus.

DARBISHIRE: But what about our train fares?

JENNINGS: We'll go by taxi. We'll get one at the station and tell him to drive to my house and my father'll pay when we get there. I live at Haywards Heath, it's only about fifteen miles away.

DARBISHIRE: But I live at Cricklewood; that's miles; it'd cost about a hundred pounds by taxi.

JENNINGS: When we get to my home, my father'll lend you some cash and then you can go home by train.

DARBISHIRE: Coo, yes. P'raps I could go in a Pullman and we might have one of those super streamlined engines...

JENNINGS: Never mind that, yet. Are you coming?

DARBISHIRE: Well, okay, then, if you think it'll be all right.

JENNINGS: We could go now; there's no one about, they're all in the Assembly Hall. Come on.

Fade to:

JENNINGS: I say, Darbishire, your eyesight must be rotten, - I mean ozard. I can't see a thing through your glasses.

DARBISHIRE: I can't see a thing without them.

JENNINGS: Here you are, you'd better have them back... Gosh, we've walked right past the bus stop and I never saw.

DARBISHIRE: That must be what I bumped into just now. I can see it now I've got my glasses.

JENNINGS: Let's go back to it and if anyone comes along we can nip behind the hedge.

DARBISHIRE: D'you think we need go on limping as there's no one about? It's awfully tiring.

JENNINGS: Well, p'raps as there's no one coming... oh, golly, there is. Look, it's a man; he's come out of the school gates. Quick, get behind the hedge!

DARBISHIRE: Who is it?... Oh!

JENNINGS: Shut up, you fool.

DARBISHIRE: But I'm kneeling on a nettle.

JENNINGS: Keep your head down, you idiot... Oh, Lord, it's Mr. Carter... He's coming this way; lie down and don't move.

Footsteps approach and recede

DARBISHIRE: Has he gone?

JENNINGS: Yes, he's going down the road. Jolly good job he didn't see us. He's gone round the corner now.

DARBISHIRE: Good, can I get off my nettle, then?... I think I can hear the bus coming.

Bus in the distance and approaching

JENNINGS: Come on then, let's nip out and stop it... Yes, and when we overtake Mr. Carter we must crouch down very low in our seats so he won't see us go past.

Bus stops: bell rings and bus starts

JENNINGS: Go right up to the front, Darbishire. You needn't go on limping now.

DARBISHIRE: I wasn't; I stumbled.

JENNINGS: Sit down; that's right. We'll be passing Mr. Carter any minute now... Yes, there he is... quick crouch down.

Bus slows down

DARBISHIRE: What are we stopping for? I must have a squint... Oh, I say, Jennings; it's Mr. Carter. He's holding his hand up to stop the bus. Oh, golly!

JENNINGS: Get down, you fool;... yes, you're right; we're stopping.

Bus stops; bell rings and bus starts; hold bus under.

The boys' dialogue is whispered

JENNINGS: Mr. Carter's got on the bus; he's sitting right at the back.

DARBISHIRE: Oh golly, we shouldn't have done this. There'll be an awful row. My father says, "Oh what a tangled web we weave..."

JENNINGS: He hasn't seen us; he's reading a newspaper. If those two fat ladies don't move, he won't know we're here. What were you saying?

DARBISHIRE: I was saying "Oh what a tangled web we weave, when first we..."

JENNINGS: Oh, shut up. We're in an awful jam and you start saying proverbs.

JENNINGS: Shut up, you fool.
DARBISHIRE: But I'm kneeling on a nettle.

DARBISHIRE: It's only what my father...

JENNINGS: Listen. We'll sit well forward and keep our heads down till Mr. Carter gets off. Then we'll be all right.

DARBISHIRE: Yes, but supposing he doesn't...

CONDUCTOR: Fares, please.

JENNINGS: (*low whisper*) Two halves to the station, please.

CONDUCTOR: Eh?

JENNINGS: Two halves to the station.

CONDUCTOR: What's the matter chum, laryngitis?

JENNINGS: (*hoarsely*) Yes.

CONDUCTOR: Can't yer pal talk, neither? Where you going, son?

DARBISHIRE: (*whispering*) Station.

CONDUCTOR: Two sore throats to the station; tanner each.

Punches tickets

I thenkyow.

Bus slows and stops

CONDUCTOR: (*calling*) 'Thampton Road. Hurry along, please.

Bell rings; Bus starts; Hold under:

DARBISHIRE: Is it all right?

JENNINGS: He's still reading his paper. I hope he gets off soon.

Fade out bus: pause: then fade in again: bus slows and stops:

CONDUCTOR: (*calling from rear*) Station! Station!

DARBISHIRE: Oh golly, we can't get out; he's still there.

JENNINGS: We'll just have to go on a bit further.

CONDUCTOR: Station! Hey, chum didn't you want the station?

JENNINGS: Don't take any notice.

CONDUCTOR: Oi! (*Whistles*) Station!

JENNINGS: Don't look round. Pretend you haven't heard.

CONDUCTOR: (*approaching*) You lads deaf as well as dumb?

JENNINGS: (*whisper*) We're going a bit further.

CONDUCTOR: Okay.

Bell rings; bus starts; hold under:

How far you going?

JENNINGS: I don't know yet.

CONDUCTOR: Better drop you at the 'ospital and get them throats looked at. What you want? Tuppeny?

JENNINGS: Yes, please.

DARBISHIRE: Oh gosh, we haven't got any more money.

CONDUCTOR: You'll have to get orf, then, won't you?

JENNINGS: But we can't get off. You don't understand. Look, couldn't I send it on to you; I'll give you my address.

CONDUCTOR: I've 'eard that one before... Well, c'mon. Are you going to 'ave another ticket, or ain't yer?

JENNINGS: (*desperate and near tears*) No, no,... wait a minute...

CONDUCTOR: Make up your mind. I ain't got all day. Either you...

MR. CARTER: Can I be of any assistance?

JENNINGS: Oh, sir!

DARBISHIRE: Oh, golly!

CONDUCTOR: It's these lads, sir. Acting a bit queer; I want another two-pence from both of 'em.

MR. CARTER: Here you are, then.

CONDUCTOR: I thenkyow.

Punches tickets

MR. CARTER: Would you mind stopping? I think we've all gone quite far enough.

Fade out bus. Pause

MR. CARTER: And now we shall have to catch a bus going the other way. Still, these little trips pass the time quite pleasantly. It was kind of you to invite me to come.

JENNINGS: What do you mean, sir?

MR. CARTER: You practically invited me when you told me you were going.

JENNINGS: But we didn't tell you, sir; how did you know, sir?

MR. CARTER: I'm not quite such a fool, Jennings. Agitated looks and whispered confabs followed by requests for large sums of money always interest me. And when this is followed by Jennings and Darbishire limping and groping blindly down the drive... I'm glad you've got your glasses back again, Darbishire; you looked quite lost without them.

JENNINGS: Did you see us then, sir?

MR. CARTER: I'm afraid I couldn't help it. And next time you hide behind a hedge, remember it's useless to put your head down if you leave your other end sticking up. But you were very good on the bus. I don't like people chattering when I'm trying to read.

JENNINGS: I...we...we're awfully sorry, sir. Will there be an awful row, sir?

MR. CARTER: Oh, I don't know; we all make mistakes. The best thing to do is to try and profit by them.

DARBISHIRE: Sir... shan't we be expelled, sir?

MR. CARTER: Why, Darbishire, would you mind very much?

DARBISHIRE: I... I'd rather like it, sir.

MR. CARTER: I thought that was probably the trouble; we all start off by feeling homesick. It's just one of those things that have to be mastered.

JENNINGS: It's not only that, sir.

MR. CARTER: Oh? What else is the matter?

JENNINGS: Well, sir, I'm going to be...oh!

MR. CARTER: Yes?

JENNINGS: I can't tell you, sir. It'd be sneaking, sir. You said last night you didn't listen to that sort of thing.

MR. CARTER: In that case, I can't press you, can I?

DARBISHIRE: I think Jennings ought to tell you, sir. My father says that circumstances alter cases.

MR. CARTER: Very true, Darbishire, but I think it might be better if Jennings could find his own salvation. Do you think that's possible, Jennings?

JENNINGS: No, sir. If I go back to school, I'll get... oh, well, I don't care.

MR. CARTER: Good. Now, if you'll wait here a moment, I'll go and enquire about a bus back.

JENNINGS: Yes, sir. (*Pause*) I say, Darbishire, he's jolly decent really, isn't he?

DARBISHIRE: Yes, I thought he'd kick up no end of a fuss. We're lucky he isn't the one who goes red in the neck.

JENNINGS: Lucky!! What about my bashing-up?

DARBISHIRE: Are you frightened?

JENNINGS: Well, just a bit. So'd you be.

DARBISHIRE: Tell Benedick. Go on, tell him. He'd soon stop it.

JENNINGS: I know he would, but I can't. What would he think? No, I've got to find my own way out, only it's not so... I say, Darbi, look at that shop over the road!

DARBISHIRE: That sweet shop?

JENNINGS: Yes; Velenti's, it's called, and they've got Brighton Rock in the window.

DARBISHIRE: I don't feel much like sweets at the moment, thanks.

JENNINGS: But don't you remember what they said in the dorm? That's the shop that Temple went into when he foxed into town last term.

DARBISHIRE: Well, you don't expect me to get excited over that, do you ?

JENNINGS: No, but I am. I can see how to... oh, blow, we haven't got any money.

MR. CARTER: (*approaching*) There's a bus in ten minutes; we'll be back by bed time and then it'll be chin up and face it.

JENNINGS: Yes sir. Sir, you know you said I'd have to settle this, er, this thing by myself?

MR. CARTER: Yes.

JENNINGS: Well, sir, I think I could do it, sir, if I could buy some of that rock in that shop over there.

MR. CARTER: But you've got plenty of tuck, haven't you?

JENNINGS: Yes, sir, but that won't do. It's got to be Brighton Rock and it's got to be in one of Valenti's paper bags with the name on it.

MR. CARTER: Well, if you're quite certain that's what you want, we'll have to make further inroads on your bank. Here you are.

JENNINGS: Thank you, sir.

MR. CARTER: What about sweet coupons?

JENNINGS: Oh Lord, I hadn't thought of that, sir. It's no good, is it? I can't get any.

MR. CARTER: Is this rock very important?

JENNINGS: Yes, sir, it's vital, sir. Everything'll be all right if I can get some. Really, sir.

MR. CARTER: H'm. I've got some sweet coupons in my pocket that were handed in to me just before lunch. But they belong to... yes, here they are. They're Temple's... I suppose we might borrow one if we are very careful to pay it back.

JENNINGS: I'll do that sir. I shall be only too glad to pay Temple back. Oh, thank you, sir.

Fade to buzz of conversation in dormitory and hold under:

ATKINSON: Venables, you dirty slacker, you haven't washed your feet.

VENABLES: Yes, I have, then, so snubs to you, Atkinson. I've only got my teeth to do.

Gear change gargling

TEMPLE: Where are those new kids? They should have been up ten minutes ago?

VENABLES: I didn't see them at tea, either. I say, Bod, weren't you going to bash one of them up before tea?

TEMPLE: Gosh, I forgot all about Jennings. If he wasn't such an ozard little oik, he'd have come and reminded me. I'll do it tomorrow; no flowers, by request; here lies Jennings, R.I.P.

JENNINGS: Who's taking my name in vain?

ATKINSON: Golly, where have you two been? The dorm bell went hours ago.

VENABLES: And where were you at tea? You missed some super wizard muck; Shepherd's Pie; I had four helpings.

TEMPLE: I suppose you were hiding from me, Jennings?

JENNINGS: Good Lord, no. I never gave you a thought, Temple. As a matter of fact, Darbishire and I foxed out. We went into town on a bus.

TEMPLE: You what?... You never did.

JENNINGS: Yes, didn't we Darbishire?

DARBISHIRE: That's right; we went out disguised like Edward G. Robinson... something. It was super!

ATKINSON: And you cut tea as well! Gosh, rare, wizzo! There'd have been an awful row if you'd been caught!

JENNINGS: I couldn't have cared less. I'm that sort, really. Darbishire's a bit of a desperado in his way, too.

ATKINSON: 'Course he is. I think you're both wizard plucky.

VENABLES: So Bod isn't the only one after all. Good old Jennings, you're rare!

TEMPLE: They're just making it up. I bet you can't prove it. Go on, prove it.

JENNINGS: Certainly. Have a bit of Brighton Rock, Bod. Here you are; I got it at Valenti's. Sorry to pinch your idea, but we improved on it rather, with our disguises. It was just as well we had them too 'cos Benedick got on the bus.

OMNES: What!!!

JENNINGS: Oh, yes, but we kept our heads.

VENABLES: Coo, rare! And you didn't get nabbed?

JENNINGS: Well, here we are to tell the tale. Have a bit of rock, Atkinson; it's genuine all right. See the name on the bag.

ATKINSON: Coo, thanks, Jennings.

JENNINGS: Hand it all round, Darbishire. Venables, want a bit?

VENABLES: Coo, thanks, Jennings... I say, Jennings, you can share my basin if you like; you and Darbishire.

ATKINSON: No, have mine, Jennings. Go on, and you can go first.

DARBISHIRE: Well, that's awfully decent of you, Atkinson. My father says that a generous impulse...

JENNINGS: Don't be so modest, Darbishire... No, I think we'll have Bod's basin.

TEMPLE: Well, -er, -yes, all right, Jennings.

JENNINGS: Darbishire and I'll wash first and then you.

TEMPLE: Well... okay, Jennings.

JENNINGS: And no rot about bashing up, eh, Bod?

TEMPLE: No, Jennings, of course; I was only joking.

JENNINGS: And I say, Bod; you don't mind me calling you Bod, do you, Bod?

TEMPLE: No, that's all right, Jennings.

JENNINGS: Well, I'm a bit fagged out after foxing into town. You might clean the basin out for Darbishire after I've washed my feet in it, will you?

TEMPLE: Yes, Jennings... Okay, Jennings.

JENNINGS
AND THE POISONOUS SPIDER

(First series no.2)

Jennings and the Poisonous Spider was the second Jennings play.

It was first broadcast by the BBC Home Service for Children's Hour on 6th November 1948, with the following cast:

MR. WILKINS	Wilfred Babbage
MR. CARTER	Geoffrey Wincott
JENNINGS	David Page
DARBISHIRE	Loris Somerville
TEMPLE	Derek Rock
ATKINSON	John Cavanah
VENABLES	John Bishop
OLD ROBO	Laidman Browne

Door knob turns loudly, followed by door slam

MR. WILKINS: (*approaching noisily*) I've just about had enough of that…

MR. CARTER: Really, Wilkins, must you always come into the staff room like a herd of buffalo thundering across the plain?

MR. WILKINS: You'd be feeling a bit frantic if you'd just had Form 3, two lessons running. I can tell you, Carter, that form's turning my hair grey. Can't behave, will talk, won't work, must fidget. I've been shouting myself hoarse in there all morning.

MR. CARTER: That's probably the trouble. Ever tried talking quietly? You see, Wilkins, if you rampage around a classroom like a bull in a china shop, they just think it's most frightfully funny.

MR. WILKINS: Nonsense; I've got to make myself felt. The whole trouble is I'm too easy with them. Take a boy like Jennings; his geometry this morning was a perfect disgrace. He'd been fencing with his ruler till it had an edge like a bread knife, he'd been playing darts with his compass till the point had gone, and on top of that he'd cut a slice out of his protractor to make a windscreen for his model fire engine.

MR. CARTER: And what did you do? Put a stripe in his conduct book?

MR. WILKINS: Yes, and a fat lot that worried him. What he needs is… I tell you, Carter, I haven't got enough authority in this place. If only I could give them a punishment that'd really make them sit up.

MR. CARTER: Such as?

MR. WILKINS: I don't know, but it'd have to be drastic; something to show them I'm a chap to be reckoned with. And, by jove, if I do think of something, that form's going to get it in the neck.

MR. CARTER: I can't help thinking you're going the wrong…

Telephone bell rings

Wait a minute.

Receiver picked up

Hallo, Linbury Court School... Yes, Carter speaking... Oh, hallo Parkinson; are you bringing a strong team over tomorrow?... Oh, sorry to hear that; yes, very disappointing... I think it's fourteen days for german measles... We'll fix it up later in the term, then. Thanks for letting me know. Goodbye.

Receiver replaced

That was Bracebridge School. We'll have to cancel tomorrow's match; they're in quarantine till next week, for german measles.

MR. WILKINS: Pity, I was looking forward to giving them a hiding. Still, if the game's scratched... Good lord, yes; why not? It's an answer to prayer.

MR. CARTER: What is?

MR. WILKINS: Now I've got Form 3 where I want them. Any more nonsense from them and I'll cancel the match with Bracebridge tomorrow.

MR. CARTER: But it's cancelled already; I've just told you, they're in quarantine.

MR. WILKINS: Yes, I know that; but they don't. That's the weapon I wanted. The first bit of trouble I get, I'll say, "Right; the whole lot of you will stay in tomorrow and there'll be no cricket match."

MR. CARTER: But you can't do that, it's not cricket. I mean, it's making out you've got the power to...

MR. WILKINS: Now, listen Carter; I shan't really be punishing them at all, because they couldn't have a match tomorrow in any case. Mind you, I was looking forward to the game as much as the boys, but if it's off anyway, why shouldn't I use it to my advantage?

MR. CARTER: I don't like the idea; it's... it's unscrupulous. Besides, they might all behave so well that you don't want to punish them.

MR. WILKINS: Is that likely? You don't know what I have to go through with that lot. And the trouble I take with them. Talk about casting pearls before...

Bell rings. Hold under:

End of break. I've got them again next lesson and, by jove, I'm going into Form 3 looking for trouble.

MR. CARTER: Don't slam the...

Door slam. Fade out bell

TEMPLE: What's the next lesson, Venables?

VENABLES: Geog, with Wilkie. He'll probably be in a super bait; I did the wrong prep.

JENNINGS: Never mind; Bracebridge match tomorrow.

ATKINSON: Wizzo.

JENNINGS: Wham! Wheeeeew! Doyng! That's me hitting one on to the roof of the pav.

TEMPLE: Swanking again, Jennings.

ATKINSON: Yes, I'd like to see him do it.

JENNINGS: Well, I'm better than you, Bod. I must be; I've seen the Australians play. I'm going to play for Surrey when I grow up.

TEMPLE: Rotten old Surrey; Surrey's ozard. I stick up for Sussex.

JENNINGS: Why?

TEMPLE: Why? Well, er... my godmother nearly went to live at Brighton.

JENNINGS: That's a daft reason.

TEMPLE: It isn't; besides I used to know a song about Sussex by the sea. So I've more right to be Sussex than you have to be Surrey.

JENNINGS: Well, if it comes to that, Bod, I know a song about Surrey; something about a fringe on the top.

DARBISHIRE: My mother's got a carpet sweeper called the "Northampton Cleaner" so I think I'm entitled to stick up for...

TEMPLE: Shut up, Darbishire; nobody asked you.

VENABLES: Cave, Wilkie.

MR. WILKINS: (*approaching noisily*) Get out your Geography prep; I want to have a look at it.

VENABLES: Did we have to write it in our books, sir?

MR. WILKINS: Where else would you expect to write it? On the ceiling? Jennings, bring your essay up... My goodness, what writing; look at your pen; two inches long with an end like a paint brush. Have you been chewing it again?

JENNINGS: Only when I get absorbed in thought, sir.

MR. WILKINS: We'll see how much thought you've put into "Wheat Farming in Australia". *(Reading)* In Austeralia there is wheat but the rabits are a pest like rats the farmers get very cross because the rabits eat the wheat, in England rabits are not a pest you can have chinchilla and angora mine was white with some brown on his name was Bobtail and I got a tea chest and put straw down. *(Finish reading)* Of all the muddle-headed... what d'you mean serving me up with nonsense like this?

JENNINGS: But, sir, it's not nonsense, it's true; my rabbit was like that. My uncle gave him to me for...

MR. WILKINS: But I set an essay on Australian Wheat-growing, not the life story of some wretched animal.

JENNINGS: Bobtail, his name was, sir.

MR. WILKINS: I don't care if his name was Moses; it's not geography; it's... it's...

DARBISHIRE: My father would say it's not germane to the issue, sir.

MR. WILKINS: That's enough, Darbishire. You illiterate nitwit, Jennings, don't you see?... This is a perfect example of, er, of...

DARBISHIRE: Juvenile delinquency.

MR. WILKINS: Be quiet, Darbishire, nobody asked you. You're half asleep, Jennings, that's your trouble; you need waking up. Go and put your head under the tap in the washroom.

JENNINGS: What, now, sir?

MR. WILKINS: Yes, now. Perhaps you'll come back a bit brighter. Go on. Now then, let's hear your essay, Darbishire.

DARBISHRE: Yes sir. H'm. *(Reading)* The vast undulating plains of Australia, pitiably bare of all foliage, bar undergrowth, stretch with pertinacity beyond the horizon to present a continuous panorama of grandiose scenery. In the declining rays of the setting sun the observer is entranced to behold...

MR. WILKINS: Wait a minute. Did you copy this out of a book?

DARBISHIRE: Only one or two bits, sir.

MR. WILKINS: And what about the wheat-growing?

DARBISHIRE: I get to that on page thirteen, sir. This is just put in to put the reader in the right mood.

MR. WILKINS: It's putting me in a mood, Darbishire, but it's not the one you're aiming at.

Door opens

You've been very quick, Jennings. Come here. Did you put your head under the tap as I told you?

JENNINGS: Yes, sir.

MR. WILKINS: Then would you mind explaining to me why your hair is quite dry?

JENNINGS: Well, sir, you never told me to turn the tap on.

Hilarious mirth, disturbance and general

pandemonium from whole class

ATKINSON: Oh, sir, isn't Jennings smashing, sir? Super wizzo.

TEMPLE: You asked for that one, sir. A real priority prang.

DARBISHIRE: He was more awake than you thought, sir. It was most hefty rare.

VENABLES: Sir, you should have told him to turn the tap on, sir.

ATKINSON: Sir, did you forget to tell him to turn the tap on, sir?

VENABLES: If you didn't actually tell him to turn the tap on, sir, he wouldn't know he had to...

MR. WILKINS: Silence... I have never in all my life heard such an exhibition of hooliganism. If that is your idea of being clever, Jennings...

TEMPLE: But it was only what you told him to do, sir.

MR. WILKINS: Quiet! And as the rest of the form obviously appreciate your type of humour, they'll have to suffer for it. The whole class will come in here for two hours detention tomorrow afternoon.

WHOLE CLASS: Oh, sir!

DARBISHIRE: But, sir, not tomorrow, sir, we can't; there's a match.

ATKINSON: Yes, sir, we're playing Bracebridge tomorrow, sir.

MR. WILKINS: You are not playing Bracebridge tomorrow. You can consider the match cancelled.

JENNINGS: Oh, but sir, you can't do that, sir, really.

MR. WILKINS: You heard what I said; I've warned you and you took no notice. Very well; no match.

WHOLE CLASS: Oh, sir!

DARBISHIRE: Supposing we behave most frightfully decently from now on, sir, won't you let us off?

MR. WILKINS: I'm not prepared to argue; I mean what I say.

TEMPLE: You are a fool, Jennings.

WHOLE CLASS: (*derisively*) Jen-nings!

ATKINSON: You rotten dago; you did it on purpose.

VENABLES: Yes, why couldn't you do what you were told?

JENNINGS: Well, you thought it was funny, anyway.

VENABLES: I never did; I thought it was just too putrid for words.

TEMPLE: It would be Jennings to get the match cancelled.

MR. WILKINS: And now, perhaps, we can get on with the lesson.

JENNINGS: Sir, it was all my fault, sir. Can I do the detention and you let the others off?

MR. WILKINS: No, Jennings.

JENNINGS: But, sir, it's not fair to them. Please let them have the match, sir, and I'll stay in and I'll go back and get my head wet, too.

MR. WILKINS: I am not in the habit of having my decisions questioned by insignificant little boys. And now, Darbishire, will you continue to read your *magnus opus*.

DARBISHIRE: My what, sir?

MR. WILKINS: That was Latin, Darbishire, meaning your great work.

DARBISHIRE: I knew what you meant, sir, only you should have said *magnum*; *opus* is neuter.

MR. WILKINS: Uh? Yes, of course; slip of the tongue. Get on with it, anyway.

DARBISHIRE: (*reading*) The vast undulating plains of Australia, pitiably bare of all foliage, bar undergrowth...

                 Fade out; pause and fade in

DARBISHIRE: Never mind, Jennings, it can't be helped. My father says that...

JENNINGS: It's jolly well not fair. I think Wilkie's as ozard as a coot.

DARBISHIRE: You can't say that; you can only be as bald as a coot.

JENNINGS: Who can?

DARBISHIRE: Anyone; it's a simile. What you meant was either Wilkie is as bald as a coot...

JENNINGS: I never said he was bald.

DARBISHIRE: No, but if you wanted to.

JENNINGS: Why should I, if he isn't? You're screwy; I said he was ozard.

DARBISHIRE: Of course, you could make up a simile and say he was as ozard as a buzzard. My father says…

JENNINGS: I bet I know what's for tea. I bet you a million pounds I do; bananas! Take me on?

DARBISHIRE: How d'you know?

JENNINGS: I can see Old Robo opening a crate by the kitchen door. I wonder if he'd let us have some of the wood. I vote we go and ask him.

DARBISHIRE: Coo, yes; I could do with some wood for my history modelling; I'm going to make a French Revolution guillotine with lashings of red ink for the blood.

Wood splitting and hammering as crates are opened

JENNINGS: I say, Robo, please d'you think we could have that banana crate when it's empty?

OLD ROBO: Ah! I'm a bit short of wood for me kindlin'.

DARBISHIRE: What's his kindling?

JENNINGS: I don't know… I say, Robo, d'you think your kindling could spare us just enough for a guillotine? Would you mind asking him, - er, her?

OLD ROBO: Ah! I got these 'ere bananas to unpack first.

Wood splitting

JENNINGS: Coo, look at the labels. That crate's come from Jamaica. (*Excited*) Coo, quick, Darbishire, look; crawling out of that bunch of bananas over there… d'you see it? A super massive spider; it's enormous.

DARBISHIRE: Golly! I've never seen one like that before; it's as big as my hand.

JENNINGS: I vote we capture it and…

OLD ROBO: Get away; don't you touch it. Poison, most like.

JENNINGS: D'you really think so? Coo, super rare.

OLD ROBO: Ah! Snakes and spiders and all them foreign reptiles is poison.

DARBISHIRE: But it'll escape and then we'll all be…

OLD ROBO: Naw. I'll just bash it one with me 'ammer.

JENNINGS: No, don't do that, Robo.

DARBISHIRE: It might be worth a lot of money. You know, a defunct species. Bags I have it. My father says...

OLD ROBO: I'll dot it one and be done with it. Catch the rabies most like if it bit yer.

JENNINGS: No, let's catch it and show it to Mr. Carter. He knows all about insects; he's a what d'you call it, - a taximeter.

DARBISHIRE: Don't be so wet, Jen. A taximeter stuffs them; Benedick's an encyclomologist.

JENNINGS: Well, let's get a move on; it's beetling off.

DARBISHIRE: How shall we catch it without getting stung, - er, bitten?

JENNINGS: Your pencil box, Darbi. You hold it open and I'll hoik it in with this bit of wood... Ready?... Golly, it can't half shift... okay, I've got it this time... there... quick, shut the lid down.

OLD ROBO: Ah! Eat its way through the box an' all, most like. I knew a chap got bit once. Arm swole right up. 'Ad to cut 'is jacket orf of 'im.

JENNINGS: What, just from a spider's bite?

OLD ROBO: Naw; snake, this was. They're all the same, them foreign reptiles; deadly, that's what.

Fade to:

DARBISHIRE: I know you saw it first, Jennings, but I bagsed it first. Besides, it's in my pencil box.

JENNINGS: Well, it can't stay there, it'll suffocate. I know, let's take it up to the dorm and put it in your tooth glass; then we can have a good dekko at it.

DARBISHIRE: Coo, yes; prang idea. Come on.

Footsteps

Couldn't we use your tooth glass?

JENNINGS: No, it's your spider; you bagsed it. You'll have to feed it too; where can we get some insects from?

DARBISHIRE: There's a fly-paper hanging up in the tuck-shop. I wonder if we could scrape some off.

JENNINGS: Here we are; this is your glass, isn't it?

Stop footsteps

DARBISHIRE: Yes.

JENNINGS: I hope he likes the smell of toothpaste. Look, I'll hold the glass and you tip him in. Then put your pencil box on the top.

DARBISHIRE: Okay. Yes, but what happens if...

JENNINGS: Oh, go on, Darbi, tip the box right up... That's right. Golly isn't he wizzo? Super hairy legs!... He looks hefty poisonous, doesn't he? I wonder if he's a... a... something like ta-ran-ta-ra.

DARBISHIRE: Tarantelle; no, that's a dance. Tarantula, that's right. Yes, of course, he must be. They're bang-on dangerous. I read a story once about some man-eating spiders; you don't think it's one of those?

JENNINGS: Might be. He seems to be drawing the line at your toothpaste, though.

DARBISHIRE: I knew a joke, too; it was putridly funny. Somebody says to somebody else, "have you heard of the man-eating spiders?" and then somebody else says to another chap, or it could be the first chap, you know, the one that somebody had said to him about the man-eating spiders, - anyway, it doesn't matter which one it is, but the other chap says, "No, but I've heard of the man eating sandwiches". Good, isn't it? Have you heard it before?

JENNINGS: No, what is it?

DARBISHIRE: I've just told you; somebody says to somebody else...

JENNINGS: Oh, that. What's funny in that? There's no such thing as a man-eating sandwich.

DARBISHIRE: Oh, you're crackers; can't even see a joke. I vote we mooch along to the libe and look it up in the encyclopaedia. Then we can find out what tarantulas eat and p'raps I'll get about a hundred pounds from the British Museum or the Zoo and we might get a medal from the R.S.P.C.A. for capturing it.

JENNINGS: And another one for saving its life from Old Robo. If it is a tarradiddle.

DARBISHIRE: Tarantula.

JENNINGS: Well, I bet it isn't, anyway. I bet you a million pounds it isn't.

DARBISHIRE: Well, I bet you two million pounds it is. Take me on?

JENNINGS: Okay; I vote we ask Mr. Carter to say.

DARBISHIRE: No fear; he'll want to collar the reward.

JENNINGS: What reward?

DARBISHIRE: There's almost bound to be one. Either it's so rare it's defunct, and professors and people'll come miles and write books about it, or if it isn't that, it'll be dangerous like the Colorado beetle and we'll get one for saving the crops.

JENNINGS: Well, if we get medals, I vote we wear them on our Sunday suits...

Fade to:

VENABLES: I say, Bod, have you heard about Darbishire? He's got a hefty smash-on spider. It's as hairy as a ruin and super lethal.

TEMPLE: Stale buns! I knew that a hundred years ago. I was there when he looked it up in the encyclopaedia.

VENABLES: What did it say?

TEMPLE: It's called something Latin; tarentula, or something.

VENABLES: I bet that's not Latin.

TEMPLE: 'Course it is; it goes like mensa. Tarentula.. tarentula.. tarentulam.. tarentulae.. tarentulae...

ATKINSON: Shut up, Bod; we don't want any Latin, now.

VENABLES: Anyway, Darbishire says it eats birds, so he's telling Old Robo not to let the hens out till the British Museum has been.

ATKINSON: Yes, and he says if it bites you, your arm swells up and they have to cut your coat sleeve to get it off. Old Robo told him.

VENABLES: Here he comes. Where've you been, Darbishire?

DARBISHIRE: If you want to know, Venables, I've been writing a letter to the British Museum. I've told them to send a man down 'cos I've got a gargantuan tarantula.

VENABLES: I thought it came from Jamaica.

DARBISHIRE: So it does; gargantuan means the size, not the place, you wet dope. The museum'll be wizard interested, I should think. They might even make me a Fellow.

TEMPLE: Jolly good!

DARBISHIRE: No, just an ordinary one. I'm a bit worried about what to feed him on, though; we can't let him catch birds. You see, the encyclopaedia wasn't quite sure; I think it's a

41

tarantula and you go nuts when it bites you, but it might be a bird-eating spider.

VENABLES: Won't it eat anything else?

DARBISHIRE: Well, I tried him with sherbet and he wouldn't even look at it.

ATKINSON: Coo, super daring. I wouldn't like to feed him.

DARBISHIRE: It's quite easy if you know anything about taxid... er.. ornith... er, if you know anything about insects. Jennings hypnotised him while I popped the sherbet in.

TEMPLE: How d'you hypnotise it?

DARBISHIRE: Jennings is rather good at it. He fixes it with a glittering eye, like the old codger in the poem who shot an albatross, Paul Revere or whatever his name was, and he stands still and doesn't move. And, by rights, the spider should have done the same, only...

Bell sounds: hold bell ringing through next sequence

VENABLES: Supper bell!

DARBISHIRE: Wizzo! I'll show it to you when we're upstairs in the dorm. It's still in my tooth glass; it makes a super observation turret...

Fade out. Door knock. Cut bell as dialogue starts

MR. CARTER: Come in.

Door opens

JENNINGS: Oh, please, Mr. Carter, sir, is Mr. Wilkins here?

MR. CARTER: You can see he isn't, Jennings. What do you want him for?

JENNINGS: Well, sir, he's cancelled the match tomorrow and it's not fair. I've offered to take the blame, but he won't listen and everybody says I'm a rotter and a cad.

MR. CARTER: I see. I'm afraid it's a matter between you and Mr. Wilkins; I can't interfere.

JENNINGS: No, sir, but do you think it's fair?

MR. CARTER: I can't answer questions like that. Mr. Wilkins will be on duty in the dormitory; you'd better see him then.

JENNINGS: Yes, sir. Er,.. sir?

MR. CARTER: Yes?

JENNINGS: Do you know a lot about taximeters, sir?

MR. CARTER: No, practically nothing; why?

JENNINGS: But I thought insects were your hobby, sir.

MR. CARTER: Insects? Oh, entomology; I know a little, why?

JENNINGS: I've got a spider here in this geometry box, sir; can you tell me if it's poisonous? Look, sir.

MR. CARTER: My word; he's a fine fellow, isn't he? Where did you come across him?

JENNINGS: In Darbishire's tooth glass, sir.

MR. CARTER: Uh? Oh yes, but before that?

JENNINGS: He came out of a crate of bananas, sir, and Darbishire's going to get the British Museum to call, but I didn't think it was a tarran-something, so I borrowed it to ask you, sir.

MR. CARTER: H'm. I'm sorry to disappoint Darbishire, but this chap's quite harmless.

JENNINGS: Isn't he even poisonous of any kind, sir?

MR. CARTER: Not even of any kind. Look, I can hold him in my hand; he's quite a common species in the West Indies. Looks rather startling, but that's all there is to it. Shall we put him back in the box?

JENNINGS: Yes, I'd better give it back to Darbishire; he doesn't know I've taken it.

Telephone bell rings

MR. CARTER: Run along now, Jennings, I'm busy.

Receiver picked up

JENNINGS: Yes, sir.

MR. CARTER: Hullo! Linbury Court here... Who? Bracebridge School... yes. You're coming here tomorrow?... But Mr. Parkinson rang up this morning and cancelled it; he said you'd had german measles... Fourteen days?... Yes, of course, if it started on the nineteenth, you'd be out of quarantine yesterday... Good; I'm so glad; we'll expect you tomorrow at two-thirty, then... Right, goodbye.

Receiver replaces

I thought I told you to go to bed, Jennings.

JENNINGS: I was just going, sir, but I thought p'raps when the phone went, you might want me to go and fetch someone, sir.

43

MR. CARTER: I see; well, good night.

JENNINGS: But sir...

MR. CARTER: What?

JENNINGS: That phone call, sir. You said Bracebridge had cancelled the match because of german measles, but Mr. Wilkins said he'd scratched it because I didn't turn the tap on and everyone made a row in class.

MR. CARTER: That was a private conversation between Bracebridge School and me.

JENNINGS: Yes, sir, but don't you see, Mr. Wilkins must have known the match was off when he said he was going to cancel it. He can't do that, sir, can he? And what'll happen tomorrow when...?

MR. CARTER: You remember what happened to the Elephant's Child with his 'satiable curtiosity? It got him into a lot of trouble.

JENNINGS: Oh, but I only stayed to be helpful, sir, in case you wanted...

Door knob rattles and door hurtles open

MR. WILKINS: (*approaching noisily*) Look here, Carter, what d'you think I ought... Oh, sorry, I didn't see you had Jennings here.

MR. CARTER: That's all right; he's going to bed now.

JENNINGS: Sir, Mr. Wilkins, sir, will you keep me in tomorrow and not the others. Honestly, sir, it wasn't their fault and they're down on me like anything.

MR. WILKINS: I'm not surprised. Go on, go to bed.

JENNINGS: But, sir, there seems to be something funny about the...

MR. CARTER: Jennings, if Mr. Wilkins said your form was to be in detention tomorrow, that's that.

JENNINGS: Yes, sir; good night, sir.

MR. CARTER: Good night, Jennings.

Door opens and shuts

By the way, Wilkins, Bracebridge have just rung up about the match. Parkinson made a mistake about the quarantine; he thought they weren't clear till Tuesday, but he's got his dates wrong, so they're coming tomorrow, after all.

MR. WILKINS: Oh, are they? And what about my detention class? I can't climb down, now.

MR. CARTER: Exactly; of course, you can still keep them in if you really want to.

MR. WILKINS: That's no good by itself; I can do that at any time. It was my being able to cancel the match that shook them.

MR. CARTER: I think you'd better find a reason to let them off.

MR. WILKINS: Yes; needs thinking out doesn't it?

Fade to:

DARBISHIRE: Come on, you chaps; if we buck up we can have a good squint at it before Wilkie gets on the prowl.

Door opens

ATKINSON: Where is it, Darbi?

DARBISHIRE: In my tooth glass. I put it on the shelf over my… Oh, golly!

VENABLES: What's the matter?

DARBISHIRE: The spider; it's gone!

ATKINSON: What!

DARBISHIRE: Yes, the gargantuan tarantula; it's escaped. Oh, corks!

TEMPLE: Don't be putrid; it can't have.

DARBISHIRE: Well, it isn't there, is it? And it was in this glass when Jennings and I left it.

VENABLES: D'you think it's crawled up the glass and squeezed out?

DARBISHIRE: Must have. Oh, golly, this is awful. It's wizard poisonous, don't forget.

TEMPLE: It must be somewhere in the dorm; we'd better try and find it. Mind out, though, if anyone sees it. Don't touch it.

ATKINSON: Supposing it rushes at us; what'll we do?

DARBISHIRE: Have to try hypnotising it. Where's Jennings? He's rare at doing that.

VENABLES: He's not up yet. Well, it's no good just standing about like a lot of spare puddings. I vote we look for it.

ATKINSON: But I'm frightened to move. I might… oh gosh, I might tread on it.

TEMPLE: Yes, it might be anywhere. In someone's pyjamas or in their bed, even.

ATKINSON: This is awful. I'm not getting into bed till it's been found.

VENABLES: Nor me. You are a dangerous maniac, Darbishire.

DARBISHIRE: How was I to know it could get out? Must have got hairy strength to shift the box like that. Come on, let's start looking and for heaven's sake don't let it bite you.

ATKINSON: No fear. Don't forget your arm swells up like a balloon and they have to cut your jacket off.

TEMPLE: I vote we all take our jackets off first, then.

VENABLES: Fat lot of good that'd be if it bit you in the foot.

DARBISHIRE: I vote we put our gum boots on in case it nips us in the ankle.

ATKINSON: All turn your beds down carefully.

Slight pause

VENABLES: Well, it's not in my pyjamas anyway, thank goodness.

DARBISHIRE: Have you looked in your bedroom slippers, Venables?

VENABLES: Yes, but I can't see right up to the end of them.

ATKINSON: Put your hand in and feel, then.

VENABLES: Oh yes, and get my finger bitten. No thank you, Atki.

DARBISHIRE: All look under your... Ooow!

TEMPLE: What's the matter?

ATKINSON: Did it get you, Darbi?

VENABLES: Are you all right? Shall I go and get Matron?

DARBISHIRE: No, it's all right; it was only a bit of fluff. Looked just like it.

TEMPLE: I don't like this; it might be anywhere; in our sponge bags, in our dressing gowns, in our towels. We may even have to get the floorboards up to find it.

ATKINSON: What are we going to do sleeping; we can't just stand up all night.

VENABLES: What else can we do? It's not safe to get undressed, let alone get into bed.

DARBISHIRE: And if we did get into bed, it might suddenly rush at us in the dark when we're asleep and we'd all wake up like swollen balloons.

TEMPLE: You ozard fool, Darbishire. Why did you have to go and... I'm going to fetch Wilkie and let him deal with it.

VENABLES: I wouldn't mind so much if it did bite him. But s'pose he can't find it?

DARBISHIRE: There's only one thing for it; we'll have to evacuate.

TEMPLE: P'raps Wilkie could get the British Museum to hurry up a bit. I'll go and find him.

DARBISHIRE: We must all keep our feet off the floor. I vote we all put our chairs in the middle of the room and stand on them. Then we can see it coming.

Chairs scraping on floor. Pause

ATKINSON: Have we got to stand like this all night?

DARBISHIRE: We might. Here comes Jennings. Come on, Jen, get your chair and bring it over here if you want to be safe. There's a super lethal prang happening.

JENNINGS: Have you all gone nuts? What are you doing up there?

ATKINSON: It's the spider, Jennings; it's got loose.

JENNINGS: Oh, is that all?

VENABLES: Don't stand there, it might charge at you.

JENNINGS: Oh phooey, I'm not frightened of a little tin-pot spider if you are.

DARBISHIRE: You're not going to get into bed, are you?

JENNINGS: 'Course I am. I'm not scared.

ATKINSON: Coo, super daring; I wouldn't.

DARBISHIRE: Mind how you turn your bed down. Golly, look out, what's that in your pyjamas? The spider's footprints!

JENNINGS: Rats! Those are cake crumbs. I foxed a hunk up to eat in bed last night.

VENABLES: You might have given me a bit.

JENNINGS: I couldn't; it went all crumbly and got all over the sheet. Massive tickly.

DARBISHIRE: Not so tickly as the tarantula'll be if it gets you.

JENNINGS: Ha! You're all a lot of funks. Who's frightened of a titchy little incey-wincey spider? I'm getting into bed.

ATKINSON: I'm staying up here till Wilkie comes.

JENNINGS: Oh corks, does Wilkie know about this?

ATKINSON: Bod's gone to fetch him.

JENNINGS: Gosh! I say, Darbishire, come over here; I want to talk to you privately.

DARBISHIRE: I daren't get down.

JENNINGS: It's urgent. Come on, you'll be all right over here. I'll convoy you.

DARBISHIRE: Okay.

JENNINGS: (*whisper*) Look, it's all right about the spider. I've got it here in my geometry box. I borrowed it to show Carter and he says it's harmless.

DARBISHIRE: Honest injun?

JENNINGS: Yes.

DARBISHIRE: Coo, what a swizz!... Oh dear, what'll the others say when they find out. They'll think I've been fooling them; I bet I get bashed up.

JENNINGS: You'd better keep quiet, then. The snag is, Wilkie'll get in a hefty bait if he knows I had anything to do with it. I'm trying to get him in a good mood so's he'll change his mind about the detention. You see, I think there may be a match after all and if we're kept in...

DARBISHIRE: What'd we better do, then?

JENNINGS: Well, the less either of us have to do with finding the spider the better. You, 'cos you'll get bashed up, and me, 'cos Wilkie'll think I pinched it just to put the wind up everybody.

DARBISHIRE: Oh golly, I wish I'd never kept the rotten thing... And I bet I don't get a reward from the British Museum.

JENNINGS: Look, I vote we put the spider on the shelf here over Temple's bed while he isn't here and then let someone find it quick before Wilkie comes.

DARBISHIRE: Okay, and we won't let on. Massive prang!

JENNINGS: I'll open the box now... there he goes!

MR. WILKINS: (*approaching noisily*) Now what's all this nonsense?

JENNINGS: Oh, gosh, here's Wilkie; let's get back to our beds.

MR. WILKINS: What are you boys doing on those chairs? Get down at once.

VENABLES: But, sir, the spider's poisonous; we might...

ATKINSON: We daren't get down, sir.

48

MR. WILKINS: Come down when I tell you. Now then, Temple, how d'you know this spider's poisonous?

TEMPLE: Darbishire looked it up in the encyclopaedia, sir; it's a tarantula that came out of a crate of bananas.

MR. WILKINS: All right; we'll take precautions; pass me that hair brush.

TEMPLE: Shall I go and fetch you a cricket bat, sir? You can have mine.

ATKINSON: No, sir, have mine; it's full size and Bod's is only a four.

VENABLES: Sir, mine's got a rubber handle, sir.

MR. WILKINS: Be quiet, all of you.

TEMPLE: If you wore batting gloves, sir, it'd be safer 'cos then you...

MR. WILKINS: Will you stop this chattering. Now then, let's have a proper search. I'll start by your bed, Temple.

TEMPLE: Oo, sir; be careful, sir.

JENNINGS: Please sir, I wanted to talk to you about that detention; I'm quite willing to stay...

MR. WILKINS: For heaven's sake, Jennings, can't you see I've got something more important to do than talk about detention. This is a serious business.

JENNINGS: Yes, sir, but this detention...

MR. WILKINS: Get back to your bed!... Well, I don't see any sign of...

TEMPLE: Ooooooh!

MR. WILKINS: What's the matter, boy?

TEMPLE: I can see it, sir.

MR. WILKINS: You can? Where? Let me get at it.

TEMPLE: No, sir; don't move, sir. Don't even bat an eyelid, sir.

MR. WILKINS: But where is it, you blithering idiot?

TEMPLE: It's on the shelf, about an inch above your head.

MR. WILKINS: Eh? What?... Dash it, I can't see it.

ATKINSON: (terrified) Sir, it's coming nearer.

VENABLES: Keep still; don't move, sir; it's your only chance or you'll swell up like a barrage balloon.

DARBISHIRE: I know; I'll throw a slipper at it.

JENNINGS: No, not you Darbishire; you're such a rotten shot you might hit Mr Wilkins.

DARBISHIRE: Well, rather be hit with a brush, than...

JENNINGS: Sir, about this detention; you must listen, really, sir, you see...

MR. WILKINS: (*rattled*) Is this a time to talk about... I wish I could see the beastly thing.

TEMPLE: You wouldn't see it from where you are, sir, it's behind my hair cream. Oh! It's coming nearer.

VENABLES: It's on the edge, now... It's taking off... Oh, sir, keep still; it's on your shoulder; it's crawling up your collar.

ATKINSON: If it bites you in the neck, sir, we'll have to cut your collar off; I'll get my nail scissors ready, shall I sir?

MR. WILKINS: What's it doing now?

DARBISHIRE: It's stopped. It's giving you a sort of look, sir.

MR. WILKINS: I'm going to knock it off with a sharp blow; stand clear, all of you.

TEMPLE: It might bite your hand, sir.

MR. WILKINS: Here, Darbishire, you looked this thing up; which end bites, the back or the front?

DARBISHIRE: All over, I think. Anyway I don't know one end from the other.

JENNINGS: It's all right, sir. Keep still and I'll get it off.

MR. WILKINS: Don't touch it, Jennings, don't touch it.

JENNINGS: But I know how to handle them, sir. I can hypnotise it... Look, I can pick it up.

OMNES: Coo!

ATKINSON: Coo... Gosh... Jennings!

TEMPLE: Holy crumpets! You've got a prang-on nerve!

VENABLES: Coo, super daring.

JENNINGS: It's all right, sir, I'll put it back in the tooth glass.

DARBISHIRE: Put the box over it. Jolly wizard show, Jennings.

TEMPLE: Yes, Jennings... Sir, he saved your life, sir.

MR. WILKINS: Thank you very much, Jennings; I'm grateful. Of course, I could have coped with it myself quite easily, but it, er, - well, it had me at a disadvantage. Very plucky of you.

MR. WILKINS: Don't touch it, Jennings, don't touch it.
JENNINGS: But I know how to handle them, sir. I can hypnotise it...

JENNINGS: That's all right, sir. It wouldn't have mattered about me, but I didn't want you to suffer, sir.

MR. WILKINS: Thank you, Jennings; it does you credit.

JENNINGS: Yes, sir... Sir, about this detention; it was my fault really and I was wondering...

MR. WILKINS: Ah, yes, of course, the detention. Well now, we've just witnessed an extremely commendable act on Jennings' part.

DARBISHIRE: Hear! Hear!

OMNES: Good old Jennings.

MR. WILKINS: So, in recognition of this er, - er,...

DARBISHIRE: Meritorious conduct.

MR. WILKINS: Be quiet, Darbishire. In recognition of this I shall cancel the detention for tomorrow afternoon.

OMNES: Coo, thank you, sir.

MR. WILKINS: And I'll go further. The match against Bracebridge will take place as arranged. The cancellation is, er, cancelled.

OMNES: Hooray! Super-duper wizzo and smash-on. Good old Jennings.

MR. WILKINS: And now, if you'll hand me that tooth glass, I'll take the beastly thing downstairs and kill it.

DARBISHIRE: Oh, no, don't do that, please, sir; it's mine.

MR. WILKINS: But it's dangerous.

DARBISHIRE: Oh, but sir, it's only... Ow! Shut up, Jennings.

JENNINGS: Sorry, Darbi, I didn't mean to tread on your toe.

MR. WILKINS: Go on, Darbishire. It's only what?

DARBISHIRE: It's only poisonous if you don't know how to handle it.

MR. WILKINS: Nonsense; it must be killed at once.

DARBISHIRE: I tell you what, sir. Let Mr. Carter put it in his butterfly killing bottle and then he can give it back to me and I can stuff it.

MR. WILKINS: Stuff it?

JENNINGS: Coo, yes, super. I know where we can get some straw.

DARBISHIRE: Straw wouldn't do for this; it'd have to be sawdust or feathers or something. Those chaps who stuff things, taxi-what d'you call them?

JENNINGS: Entomologists.

DARBISHIRE: That's right. Well, when they do stags' heads and things they use buttons or something for the eyes.

JENNINGS: Prang... pranger... prangest! I know where we can get some buttons.

MR. WILKINS: It's going to look like an odd sort of specimen by the time you've finished with it.

JENNINGS: And we can make a glass case...

Fade out. Door hurtles open

MR. WILKINS: (*approaching noisily*) Carter, will you put this ghastly insect in your killing bottle. The wretched thing nearly had me; if it hadn't been for some pretty prompt action by Jennings, I might have been done for by now.

MR. CARTER: Done for?

MR. WILKINS: Well, it's poisonous, isn't it? Here, don't touch it.

MR. CARTER: Why not? It's quite harmless. I told Jennings it was.

MR. WILKINS: You told...? You mean Jennings knew the thing was harmless all the time?... And he let me... So that was the game, was it!

MR. CARTER: I don't follow.

MR. WILKINS: He picked it off my collar. Dash it, I congratulated him on his bravery and cancelled the detention and said they could play the match tomorrow!

MR. CARTER: You'd have had to have said that, anyway; it gave you a very good excuse.

MR. WILKINS: Yes, I know, but... the beastly little boy must have been laughing at me. Right! I'll see he doesn't get away with this. Dash it!... it's.. it's deceitful.

MR. CARTER: I don't think I should take it any further, Wilkins. You see, Jennings was here when the phone message came from Bracebridge and quite by accident he found out that your scratching the match this morning was, - well, er, deceitful.

MR. WILKINS: Oh!

MR. CARTER: Quite. He's not the sort of boy to say anything if you don't, so all things considered, I think it's better to let sleeping dogs lie, don't you?

MR. WILKINS: H'm... Yes... perhaps you're right, Carter; p'raps you're right.

JENNINGS
AND THE FRIEND OF THE FAMILY

(First series no.3)

Jennings and the Friend of the Family was the third Jennings play.

It was first broadcast by the BBC Home Service for Children's Hour on 27th November 1948, with the following cast:

JENNINGS	David Page
DARBISHIRE	David Spenser
TEMPLE	Derek Rock
VENABLES	John Bishop
ATKINSON	John Cavanah
MR. RUSSELL	Eric Anderson
THE MANAGER	Charles Lefeaux
THE HEADMASTER	Laidman Browne
THE MAID	Beryl Calder
MR. CARTER	Geoffrey Wincott

Fade in:

JENNINGS: (*chanting*) Can anyone lend me something to read? Can anyone lend me something to read? This is the Jennings' Broadcasting Network. Here is an S.O.S. Can anyone lend me...

TEMPLE: Shut up, Jennings, we're trying to read. Why can't you keep quiet and get on with your library book?

JENNINGS: I can't. I've been stopped using the library. Jolly well wasn't fair.

VENABLES: Oh no! You only left a hunk of bread and jam between the pages of *Swallows and Amazons*.

ATKINSON: Yes, and I wanted it next.

JENNINGS: Well, you can still have it.

ATKINSON: What, with all the pages gummed up?

JENNINGS: It'll wash, won't it? All you want is a good stiff nail-brush. (*Chanting loudly*) Can anyone lend me something to read? Can anyone lend me something...

OMNES: Shut up, Jennings.

VENABLES: You know this is supposed to be quiet hour. If Mr. Carter hears you we'll all...

JENNINGS: I can't keep quiet if I've nothing to do.

DARBISHIRE: Come on, Jennings, you can share this magazine with me. It's chronic boring.

JENNINGS: Coo, thanks Darbishire... Oh, I've read this one.

DARBISHIRE: Let's look at the adverts then.

JENNINGS: Okay... Coo, this is rather wizard. "The Grossman Cine Camera. Motion Pictures in colour; 9 and 16mm." What's "mm"?

DARBISHIRE: It's a thing like centigrades or kilowatts; the depth or the weight of something.

JENNINGS: It'd be prang if we had one; we could make a film of the Head giving you six of the best. Pity it isn't a talkie, so's we could get the yells in too.

DARBISHIRE: And we could do a special slow motion picture of you doing your prep, and a fast motion one of you eating your tea.

JENNINGS: And don't forget the colour. We could get Mr. Wilkins into a supersonic bait and film the back of his neck turning pink. Stupendous attraction; Wilkie getting the breeze up in gorgeous technicolour! It's colossal! It's terrific! It's the picture of the century!

DARBISHIRE: Huh! Got to get your camera first. I bet they cost about a hundred pounds.

JENNINGS: Let's write for a catalogue. It says you can have one. Here, lend me your pen.

DARBISHIRE: Okay, what shall we say?

JENNINGS: Dear Mr. Grossman, - er, no, dear sir. What next? Hope you're having decent weather?

DARBISHIRE: No; say you want a catalogue and how much are the cameras.

JENNINGS: What about "I would like to buy one"?

DARBISHIRE: How much dosh have you got?

JENNINGS: Eleven and eightpence.

DARBISHIRE: Well, how can you buy it if you haven't got enough dosh?

JENNINGS: I didn't say I was going to buy it, I said I'd like to buy it. So I would.

DARBISHIRE: Yes, but he'll think...

JENNINGS: Well, if I say I'm not going to buy one, he won't send me the catalogue and it'd be a super decent thing to have.

DARBISHIRE: All right. What else? We can't just say that... Let's say what we usually do in our Sunday letters.

JENNINGS: Yes, I could tell him we beat Bracebridge School by four wickets and say we're practising for the Sports next week.

DARBISHIRE: Fat lot he'll care about that.

JENNINGS: Well, it fills up the page a bit. And then what about hoping he's quite all right, yours affectionately, J.C.T. Jennings?

DARBISHIRE: That's a rotten letter. I bet he won't send the catalogue.

JENNINGS: I know. Let's ask Temple to write it. He's got a twelve horse-power brain and he's got supersonic grown-up writing, all slopey and illiterate.

DARBISHIRE: You mean illegible.

JENNINGS: Yes, just like grown-ups... Bod, will you write a letter for me. Here it is in rough, look, only we want you to touch it up and make it more sort of grown-up.

TEMPLE: Let's have a look, then. (*Reading*) Dear Sir, I would like to buy one so how much are they please say how much the camrass but send a catlog we did sports prackstick on Wendysday. Hopping you are quit all rit. (*Stops reading*) You're crackers; what on earth does it mean?

JENNINGS: Here's the advert, look.

TEMPLE: Oh, I see... Well, what's this quit hopping stunt?

JENNINGS: It's only decent to hope he's all right. And if he isn't, - if he's got chicken-pox or something, he'll be wizard pleased to know somebody cares.

TEMPLE: I'd better write it properly. Got any decent paper?

DARBISHIRE: I've got some with Linbury Court printed on in red, and it's got the crest on and the motto in Latin. Here you are, it's spivish rare.

TEMPLE: That'll do fine. Shall I alter it to Linbury Court School?

JENNINGS: No, don't put that in. If he knows we're at school, he'll guess we don't really mean to buy one and he won't send the catalogue.

TEMPLE: Well, don't all crowd round, I can't write.

JENNINGS: Yes, get away Atkinson and Venables; it's private.

TEMPLE: Where's the address of this place; you have to write it above "Dear Sir".

JENNINGS: Why, the chap knows where he lives, doesn't he?

DARBISHIRE: It says the address in the advert; somewhere in Oxford Street.

VENABLES: Good old Oxford!

ATKINSON: Rotten old Oxford! Good old Cambridge.

JENNINGS: No they're not, then, Atkinson. Good old Oxford and snubs to you.

ATKINSON: Cambridge is miles better; it's spivish coy. Oxford on the tow-path doing up their braces; Cambridge on the river, winning all the races.

JENNINGS: No, it isn't, then; that's wrong. It's Oxford on the river winning...

TEMPLE: Shut up, Jennings and all of you; I'm trying to write a letter.

JENNINGS: Yes, shut up, you chaps; how can Bod concentrate with you making all that row. Besides, everyone knows Cambridge is ozard. Mr. Wilkins was at Cambridge, so that proves it; all twits are Cambridge.

ATKINSON: And all twerps are Oxford. I'm Cambridge, Arsenal and Lancashire.

VENABLES: Well, I'm Oxford, Charlton Athletic and Middlesex.

DARBISHIRE: And I'm Oxford...

ATKINSON: Shut up, Darbishire, no one asked you. You only say you're Oxford because Jennings does.

DARBISHIRE: No, I don't then; I've got a reason. My brother stuck up for Oxford till his last term at school and then he had the most ghastliest bit of bad luck.

VENABLES: Why, what happened?

DARBISHIRE: He won a scholarship to Cambridge.

JENNINGS: What filthy rotten luck. I bet he was fed up.

DARBISHIRE: He seemed quite pleased, actually. Spivish disloyal, I called it.

ATKINSON: You ought to be Cambridge, then, Darbi, if your brother's there.

DARBISHIRE: Well, in boat races and things, I'm Oxford first and Cambridge second.

TEMPLE: How's this for a letter. (*Reading*) Dear Sir, I am thinking of buying one of your motion picture cine cameras, (*Stop reading*) You needn't actually buy one of course, - (*reading*) and I shall be glad if you will send me your catalogue...

Fade to typewriter in distance and hold under; fade in Manager:

THE MANAGER: (*reading*) ...I am thinking of buying one of your motion picture cine cameras and I shall be glad if you will send me your catalogue as advertised. Yours truly, J.C.T. Jennings. (*Stop reading*) There you are, Mr. Russell, I told you business was looking up.

MR. RUSSELL: He certainly sounds interested. Doesn't mean to say he'll buy one, though.

THE MANAGER: I think he will if we adopt the right tactics. Now, what does Mr. Jennings' letter suggest to you?

MR. RUSSELL: That he wants a catalogue.

Fade out typewriter

THE MANAGER: No, no, no; more than that, surely. Look at it. Finest quality note-paper, with Linbury Court, Sussex in embossed letters. Sounds like a big house; plenty of money. And look at the crest! Do you have crested notepaper? No. Do I? No. Why not? Because it's the prerogative of the wealthy aristocratic families with big houses and large country estates. You'll probably find that this Mr. Jennings, - he might even be Sir J.C.T. Jennings for all we know, - you'll probably find that he's the squire of the village, rolling in money and quite willing to buy our latest model.

MR. RUSSELL: All right, then; what are we waiting for? Post him a catalogue straight away.

THE MANAGER: No, no, no, Mr. Russell. You've got to be more tactful when you're dealing with important customers. He'll expect the personal touch.

MR. RUSSELL: Very well; let's send a salesman down.

THE MANAGER: I think it would be better if you went yourself. This may be a big thing. If Mr. Jennings buys a cine camera, everybody who is anybody in his part of the country will be wanting one too.

MR. RUSSELL: Yes, I think you're right. I'll go down and see him and take our latest model and plenty of film.

THE MANAGER: And mind how you treat him; a man in his position will expect a certain amount of deference. Find out his interests; talk to him about hunting, shooting and fishing.

MR. RUSSELL: I'll manage him all right. What about my going tomorrow?

THE MANAGER: Excellent, Mr. Russell. And don't come back without selling a camera.

MR. RUSSELL: Trust me!

Fade in typewriter: bring up, then fade to school bell. Fade bell

TEMPLE: What's the next lesson, Venables?

VENABLES: Latin, with the Head. Oh, golly, we had to do hic, haec, hoc, for prep. D'you know how it goes, Jennings?

JENNINGS: It goes like a machine gun; hic-hic-hic-haec-haec-haec-hoc-hoc-hoc-hic-haec-hoc-hic-haec-hoc-hic-haec-hoc... BANG!

DARBISHIRE: Coo, yes; you could have Roman rear gunners in Caesar's Spitfire legion all blazing away in Latin. Here comes a jet-propelled feminine ablative; hac-hac-hac-hac-hac-hac-hac-hac-hac.

TEMPLE: I'm an anti-tank accusative singular; hunc-hanc-hoc; hunc-hanc-hoc.

JENNINGS: Take cover; I'm a genitive dive bomber; horum-harum-horum; horum-harum-horum.

ATKINSON: Roman wireless op. sending out Latin signals. (*Morse tempo*) hi-hae-haec; hos-has-haec; huius-huius-huius; you answer me, Venables.

VENABLES: Okay; huic-huic-huic-huic-huic-huic.

All speak simultaneously with rhythmic beat

DARBISHIRE: Hac-hac-hac; hac-hac-hac; hac-hac-hac;

TEMPLE: Hunc-hanc-hoc; hunc-hanc-hoc; hunc-hanc-hoc;

JENNINGS: Horum-harum-horum; horum-harum-horum; horum-harum-horum;

ATKINSON: Hi-hae-haec; hi-hae-haec; hi-hae-haec;

VENABLES: Huic-huic-huic; huic-huic-huic; huic-huic-huic;

All break off suddenly, except Jennings

JENNINGS: Hic...haec...hoc...B A N G!

HEADMASTER: Which boy went on talking after I came in? Come along, now, who was talking?

JENNINGS: I wasn't really what you'd call talking, sir.

HEADMASTER: Then what were you doing, Jennings?

JENNINGS: I... I spoke, sir.

HEADMASTER: You weren't talking, but you spoke. The distinction is too subtle for my simple mind.

JENNINGS: It came out by accident, sir.

HEADMASTER: Really! I'll see how much prep you've done. Have you written out your Latin?

JENNINGS: No, sir, I hadn't got a pen.

HEADMASTER: Why not?

JENNINGS: It... It broke, sir.

HEADMASTER: It broke! Of its own accord naturally. Not "I was talking" and "I broke it", but "it came out by accident and "it broke"! Most unsatisfactory and evasive, Jennings. I'll test you orally; bring up your Latin primer.

JENNINGS: Yes, sir.

HEADMASTER: What's this?... Jennings, when Mr. Kennedy wrote this admirable book, he saw fit to call it "The Shorter Latin Primer". Had he wished to call it "The Shorter Way of Eating Prime Beef", I've no doubt he would have done so.

JENNINGS: Yes, sir.

HEADMASTER: Of course, I can't hold you responsible for it. Your pen obviously decided to alter the lettering before it accidentally broke itself in half.

JENNINGS: No, sir. I did it, sir.

HEADMASTER: You surprise me. And do you know what happens to boys who scribble in text books?

JENNINGS: Yes, sir.

HEADMASTER: Let us delve between the covers, then... What's all this?

JENNINGS: You told us to write our name in the book, sir.

HEADMASTER: Your name, Jennings, yes; but I don't think that purposes of identification demand quite so much detail as this. (*Reading*) If this book should dare to roam, box its ears and send it home; to J.C.T. Jennings, Linbury Court School, Bishopstone, Sussex, England, Europe, Eastern Hemisphere, Earth, near Moon, Solar System, Space, near More Space. (*Stop reading*) That, you destructive little hooligan, is ruining a perfectly good book.

JENNINGS: Yes, sir.

HEADMASTER: And not content with that, you smear your illiterate scrawl all over the fly-sheet in ridiculous doggerel. (*Reading*) Latin is a language, as dead as dead can be. It killed the ancient Romans, and now it's killing me. (*Stop reading*) What brilliant wit! What biting satire! What a masterly condemnation of the school curriculum!

JENNINGS: I don't mean it's killing me literally, sir; you have to take the poem meteorologically.

HEADMASTER: Very illuminating. During the ten years that I've been Headmaster of this school, Jennings, I have never tolerated nasty little vandals who spoil expensive text-books. Very well; "A", you will pay five shillings for a new book and "B", you will stay in all afternoon and write your prep out six times with an unbroken pen.

JENNINGS: Yes, sir.

HEADMASTER: I am aware that the Inter House Sports are being held this afternoon and I am also aware that your house is relying on you to compete in various races. This will, perhaps, bring it home to you that boys who misbehave, punish not only themselves, but their friends and colleagues as well. I'm afraid you will not be very popular with the rest of your house.

Door knock

Come in.

Door opens

Yes? What is it, Mary?

MAID: There's a gentleman to see Mr. Jennings, sir.

HEADMASTER: Mister (!) Jennings?

MAID: That's what he said, sir, but I expect he meant Master Jennings. Mr. Russell, his name is.

HEADMASTER: I don't think I... Do you know a Mr. Russell, Jennings; is he a relation?

JENNINGS: No, sir.

HEADMASTER: Perhaps he's a friend of the family. You'd better go and see who it is.

JENNINGS: Yes, sir.

HEADMASTER: No, wait a minute. You can go through hic, haec, hoc, first. Mary, show Mr. Russell into the drawing-room; tell him Jennings is just coming and I'll be along to meet him very shortly.

MAID: Yes, sir.

Door opens and shuts

HEADMASTER: Now, Jennings.

JENNINGS: Hic, haec, hoc, hunc, hanc, hoc...

Fade to:

MAID: Will you wait a minute here in the drawing room, please, sir.

MR. RUSSELL: Ah, thank you. What a charming room! I certainly think Linbury Court is one of the finest houses I've ever seen.

MAID: Yes, sir.

MR. RUSSELL: I imagine it needs a large staff to look after a place this size.

MAID: Oh yes, there's me and three other maids and cook and four house-parlourmen and Old Robo and Mrs Barsnack and...

MR. RUSSELL: Excellent! Mr. Jennings must be a gentleman of considerable means.

MAID: (*giggling*) Mr. Jennings? Hee-hee-hee.

MR. RUSSELL: What's the matter?

MAID: Nothing, sir.

MR. RUSSELL: I suppose there's plenty of hunting, shooting and fishing and all that sort of thing?

MAID: There's no hunting; there's riding though.

MR. RUSSELL: Yes, of course; and shooting?

MAID: Yes, on the rifle range.

MR. RUSSELL: Ah, Mr. Jennings is a military type, obviously. Does he prefer to be addressed by his army rank? What is he, Colonel? Brigadier?

MAID: (*giggling*) Hee-hee-hee. No, he's not in the army... not yet. Excuse me, sir, hee-hee-hee.

MR. RUSSELL: Here, don't go; wait a...

Door shuts

MR. RUSSELL: Oh, what a nuisance; just as I...

Door knock

Come in.

Door opens

Good mor... Oh... Who are you?

JENNINGS: Please sir, I'm Jennings.

MR. RUSSELL: You're...? You mean you're Mr. Jennings' son?

JENNINGS: Yes, sir.

MR. RUSSELL: Yes, of course, but it's your father I've come to see.

JENNINGS: My father doesn't live here. He just comes down for the weekend sometimes to see me.

MR. RUSSELL: But surely, this is his address, isn't it?

JENNINGS: Good gracious no. You wouldn't expect to find him still at school at his age, would you?

MR. RUSSELL: What?... At school?... Do you mean to tell me this is a school?

JENNINGS: Yes. Linbury Court Preparatory School.

MR. RUSSELL: Good heavens! Well of all the... then you must be J.C.T. Jennings!

JENNINGS: Yes, that's right.

MR. RUSSELL: And it was you who wrote to us about the cine cameras?

JENNINGS: Oh golly, is that who you are?

MR. RUSSELL: It certainly is, and I've come all the way to sell you one.

JENNINGS: But I never meant you to come; I never asked you to. I only wanted a catalogue; the advertisement said we could have one.

MR. RUSSELL: You didn't say you were a schoolboy; you said you wanted to buy a camera.

JENNINGS: Well I still want to, only I'm a bit short of dosh, -er, money.

MR. RUSSELL: Do you know how much this camera costs? Seventy five guineas! Seventy-five guineas!... And how much have you got?

JENNINGS: Eleven and eightpence.

MR. RUSSELL: Eleven and eightpence; Cor!!!

JENNINGS: But it's my birthday next month and I usually get...

MR. RUSSELL: Listen, my boy, you've got me here under false pretences. Smart note-paper, imposing address, embossed crest, what were we to think? I've given up a whole day, cancelled important engagements and travelled sixty miles to get here. And all for what?... To be offered eleven and eightpence for a seventy-five guinea movie camera!

JENNINGS: I'm terribly sorry, Mr. Russell, but I never...

MR. RUSSELL: Sorry! I should think so. For the first time in my life, I've been taken for a mug... It's absurd... it's ridiculous! When I go back and tell the Manager I've been wasting time and money like this, he'll foam at the mouth.

JENNINGS: Coo, will he really?

MR. RUSSELL: I can just imagine what he'll say when I tell him. "Your Mr. Jennings", I'll tell him, and I can just picture his face when I say it, "your Mr. Jennings…" (*starts to chuckle and then his wrath fades in uncontrollable laughter*) Ha-ha-ha-ha… wealthy aristocrat, I'll tell him… hee-hee-hee-hee… squire of the village… everybody in Sussex who is anybody, ha-ha-ha-ha- careful how I handle important customers, ho-ho-ho-ho-; eleven and eightpence for our latest hee-hee-hee-; oh, dear, I don't know when I've laughed so much. No wonder the maid thought I was up the pole. Hunting, shooting and fishing; she must have thought I was ha-ha-ha-ha-; thank goodness I can see the funny side of it.

JENNINGS: I wish I could.

MR. RUSSELL: Well, can't you?

JENNINGS: It hasn't got a funny side for me.

MR. RUSSELL: If I can take it as a joke, with all the business I'm losing, I'm sure you can.

JENNINGS: But you don't understand; the headmaster's coming along in a minute to find out why you've come to see me.

MR. RUSSELL: Is he, by jove! He'll laugh himself silly when I tell him that…

JENNINGS: No, he won't. You don't know Headmasters; they're not made like that… And I'm in awful trouble already.

MR. RUSSELL: Why, what's up?

JENNINGS: I'm being kept in this afternoon during the sports, just because I put my name and address and a sort of poem thing in a Latin primer and everyone makes it into eating prime beef anyway. And my House were counting on me for the 220 and the Long Jump and we can't possibly win the cup otherwise and they'll probably bash me up and Mr. Carter'll give me a look and not say anything and that's worse than the bashing-up, 'cos I like him and if you let him down, it's awful.

MR. RUSSELL: I don't quite follow all that, but I gather the future outlook is cloudy.

JENNINGS: Yes and it'll be worse in a minute, 'cos the Head'll say I shouldn't have written to you and he'll think I've asked you to come down on purpose and we're not allowed to have anyone to see us except relations and friends and there'll be another row about that.

MR. RUSSELL: I see; it's as serious as all that, is it?

JENNINGS: It couldn't be any worse.

MR. RUSSELL: But if friends are allowed to visit you, that's fine. I'm a friend of yours now. We've known each other at least five minutes.

JENNINGS: I'm not sure that you'd count. You don't even know my father.

MR. RUSSELL: Well, now come to think of it, I do know a Mr. Jennings; lived at, er,- um...

JENNINGS: Haywards Heath?

MR. RUSSELL: I'm just trying to remember; it might have been.

JENNINGS: If you really knew my father, that'd make all the difference.

MR. RUSSELL: It's quite likely to be him, isn't it? Just as likely as any other Mr. Jennings, at any rate.

JENNINGS: But I don't really think... oh, but it wouldn't be very good manners to contradict you, would it, sir?

Door opens

HEADMASTER: Good morning, Mr. Er, - um...

MR. RUSSELL: Good morning. Are you the Headmaster?

HEADMASTER: Yes.

MR. RUSSELL: How d'you do; my name is Russell.

HEADMASTER: Ah, yes, Mr. Russell. Jennings, wait outside in the hall, will you.

JENNINGS: Yes, sir.

Door opens and shuts

HEADMASTER: May I enquire whether you're a relation of the Jennings family?

MR. RUSSELL: No, no, just a friend. I do a lot of business with a Mr. Jennings of... of...

HEADMASTER: Haywards Heath?

MR. RUSSELL: That name does ring a bell certainly. However, as I was in the district, I decided to call.

HEADMASTER: Very kind of you. The boys are always pleased to see friends of the family.

MR. RUSSELL: I gather you're having the Sports this afternoon. I was hoping I might be allowed to watch. I'm sure Mr. Jennings would be interested to hear a first hand account of the 220 and the Long Jump.

HEADMASTER: I'm afraid that Jennings won't be competing. A little matter of discipline, you know.

MR. RUSSELL: That's a pity. You see, I've brought my cine camera. I was just thinking what excellent material the Sports would make for a colour film. Have you got a projector?

HEADMASTER: Oh yes, we hire films quite frequently.

MR. RUSSELL: But how much more satisfying to show a film you'd made yourself.   I was thinking of something like this. Caption; Linbury Court School Inter House Sports. Then a long shot of the grounds with the school in the distance; the coloured flags fluttering gaily in the breeze; the sun streaming down and the boys streaming out in their bright blazers... Medium shot of the runners lining up for the start... Close-up of the starter's finger on the trigger of the gun; they're off... Crowd scene of excited technicoloured spectators shouting themselves hoarse... Camera pans back to the runners; number 3 trips up and number 5 crashes down on top of him... Number 4's in the lead... Close-up of his determined expression... Camera tracks to the finishing tape... Medium shot of the judges trying to look calm beneath their mounting excitement... Close-up of the stop-watch, the second hand ticking remorselessly on... Cut; back to the running track... Photo-finish of the result... Smiling winner slapped on the back by admiring friends... Then the cup being presented by the Headmaster, the sunlight picking out the colours of his academic hood... What an idea for a picture!... It's an inspiration!... It's a masterpiece!

HEADMASTER: You're right, Mr. Russell, it is! A permanent record to thrill ensuing generations of boys and to recapture the memories of old boys visiting their alma mater forty years on, when afar and asunder, parted are those who are...

MR. RUSSELL: Quite... What a pity it's just an idle dream.

HEADMASTER: Idle dream? But, Mr. Russell, you suggested... that is, if you've brought your camera specially, this is just the opportunity.

MR. RUSSELL: On second thoughts, I think I'd better be getting back to town.

HEADMASTER: Oh, but surely...

MR. RUSSELL: It's like this, Headmaster. The reason I came down with my camera was to see our friend Jennings. I had hoped to interest him in... but that's another story. However, if he's being kept in this afternoon, he won't be able to appear in the film.

HEADMASTER: That's a pity, of course, but I'm sure the rest of the school will provide adequate material.

MR. RUSSELL: I'd rather not, if you don't mind. If Jennings could be in it it'd be different, but I think the family would be disappointed if he wasn't in the picture; he usually is, I should think. Well, I'm glad to have met you. Do you know how often the trains run back to town?

HEADMASTER: Now, just a moment, Mr. Russell. Perhaps I was a little hasty; but defacing books is a serious matter. Excuse me.

Opens door

Come in, Jennings. H'm. For the sake of your House, Jennings, and because Mr. Russell has come all this way to see you, I have decided to allow you to compete in the Sports this afternoon.

JENNINGS: Yes, sir; thank you, sir.

HEADMASTER: You will, of course, pay for the book out of your school bank and do your written imposition this evening.

JENNINGS: Thank you very much, sir.

HEADMASTER: Mr. Russell has kindly offered to make a film of this afternoon's proceedings. Now, as a title, I suggest Sports Day at Linbury and underneath that, some apt quotation from the classics, such as, er,- Hic... Hic... How does it go? Hic...

MR. RUSSELL: Hickory-dickory-dock?

JENNINGS: Hic, haec, hoc?

HEADMASTER: No, no; ah, I have it. Hic dies, vere mihi festus, atras eximet curas.

MR. RUSSELL: Come again?

HEADMASTER: This day, in truth a holiday to me, shall banish idle cares. Horace, Book 3, Ode number 14.

MR. RUSSELL: Just as you say, Headmaster; I won't dispute it. And after all that, we should have a credit title. This film appears by kind permission of the Grossman Cine Camera Company, Ltd.

JENNINGS: And there's one more we ought to have, too, Mr. Russell.

MR. RUSSELL: What's that?

JENNINGS: Jennings appears by kind permission of the Headmaster.

Fade out. Fade in ringing of hand bell

ATKINSON: Sir, what are you ringing the bell for, sir?

MR. CARTER: So that the chattering throng will stop talking, Atkinson, and listen to the events being announced.

JENNINGS: Oh, sir, Mr. Carter, sir, can I be bell ringer, sir?

MR. CARTER: All right, Jennings; I hereby appoint you official director of campanology.

JENNINGS: Does that mean I do the tinkles on the blower? Oh, wizard.

ATKINSON: What can I be, sir?

MR. CARTER: You, Atkinson, can be chief salvage officer and deputy armourer.

ATKINSON: Coo, thank you, sir. Thanks most frightfully, sir... Er, what does it all mean, sir?

MR. CARTER: It means that when I fire the starting pistol, you are the used cartridge-case picker-upper.

ATKINSON: I see, sir. Do you have to use a pistol to start all the races, sir?

MR. CARTER: What would you expect me to use, - a bow and arrow?

ATKINSON: Ah, but you don't use a gun for high jump, sir, I got you there, sir, didn't I, sir?

MR. CARTER: You'll be for the high jump if you go on asking silly questions. I'm going over for the high jump, now; ring the bell, Jennings.

Bell rings.

Fade in Mr. Carter, distant, announcing through megaphone:

MR. CARTER: High Jump, under 12... High Jump, under 12.

TEMPLE: That means 440's next. Are you in that, Jennings?

JENNINGS: No, but Darbishire is; have you seen him anywhere, Bod?

TEMPLE: No... Yes, there he is; golly, look at him. He's wearing his raincoat on top of his overcoat and his travelling rug over that.

JENNINGS: What's up Darbishire; got pneumonia?

DARBISHIRE: (*gasping*) No, but I'll probably get heat-stroke any minute now. I've got two sweaters on under this.

JENNINGS: Whatever for?

DARBISHIRE: Well, there's a smash-on book on Athletics in the library and it says the muscles are stimulated to greater degrees of activity by the maintenance of an optimum body-heat. So I'm maintaining the optimum.

JENNINGS: What's that mean?

DARBISHIRE: It means it's spivish hot inside all this clutter. I shan't run in it though.

JENNINGS: I read that book; it's prangish rare; it tells you to eat a lot of fruit.

DARBISHIRE: I know; I've eaten seven apples and a pound of plums in the last half hour, but I don't feel I could run much faster. Thank goodness I've got ten yards start.

JENNINGS: And you'll need it. Everyone else can run ten times as fast as you.

DARBISHIRE: Yes, but that's all right, Jennings, 'cos if they run ten times as fast as me, when they've run ten yards, I shall be a yard in front with my start.

JENNINGS: They'll soon catch that up.

DARBISHIRE: Well, I've worked out a theory that they won't. 'Cos when they've run that yard, I'll be a tenth of a yard in front; and when they've gone that tenth, I shall be a hundredth of a yard in front; and then a thousandth and then a ten-thousandth and then... well, they'll never be able to catch me up, will they? I drew a graph so that proves it.

JENNINGS: But that's crackers.

DARBISHIRE: Well, if they do catch me up it proves that Arithmetic is all wrong and it's just a waste of time learning it.

JENNINGS: Gosh, they've finished the high jump. I must ring the bell. Mr. Carter said that I was in charge of the camp theology.

Bell rings

MR. CARTER: (*through megaphone*) 440 yards under 12. Nuttall, Temple, Darbishire, Bromwich Major, Martin-Jones. (*Stop using megaphone*) Now this isn't a sprint, so take it easy to start with. There are two laps and you must keep this side of the flags, especially when you're out of sight behind the bowling-screen. Now, then, on your marks... get set...

Starting pistol fired

VENABLES: They're off! Wizzo. Go on, Temple; I bet Temple wins. Who d'you stick up for, Jennings?

JENNINGS: Darbishire, of course, but he hasn't got an earthly; he runs like a crab with chilblains. He's supersonic at the egg and spoon, though. Here comes the Head and Mr. Russell; he's hefty decent. I hope the Head won't ask him too many questions, though.

HEADMASTER: That's excellent, Mr. Russell; your shots of the high jump will be an inspiration for years to come. Ah, Jennings, there you are; you must certainly write and tell your father how pleased we are that Mr. Russell came down to see you today. Or perhaps, Mr. Russell, you'll be seeing Mr. Jennings yourself. I suppose you see him quite often?

MR. RUSSELL: Well, er, as a matter of fact, er, - oh, look, they're coming into view round the bowling-screen. I must get a shot of this. Excuse me!

Fade in cheering, hold a moment and fade out

JENNINGS: Here they come; they're on the second lap now. Temple's leading, Martin-Jones second, then Bromwich Major and Nuttall. Oh, golly, Darbishire's about twenty miles behind.

VENABLES: Last lap, Temple, go it! Go on, Jonah! Go on Bromo ma(y); go it Nutty!

HEADMASTER: This is going to be a good race, Mr. Carter; and we shall have a first rate pictorial record, thanks to Mr. Russell. I'm learning quite a lot about film photography, too. Did you notice how he crouched down on the ground to take pictures of the high jumpers? That's called tracking, - or is it panning? – anyway, it's most interesting. Ah, there's Temple disappearing round the bowling-screen for the second time. They're all very close together, aren't they?

MR. CARTER: All except Darbishire; he's still on the first lap.

HEADMASTER: Where's Mr. Russell? We must have some pictures of the finish.

VENABLES: Here they come! Go on, Temple; Jonah's just behind you!

Fade in short burst of cheering

ATKINSON: Hurray! Good old Temple! He's won. Spivish rare race! What's the next one?

MR. CARTER: (*through megaphone*) 220 yards, under 12.

VENABLES: Come on, Jennings, we're in the 220.

MR. CARTER: Venables, Atkinson, Garstang Minor, Voysey and Jennings. Are you all ready?... Jennings, what on earth are you doing with that trowel?

JENNINGS: I'm digging footholes to get a good start, sir. The book said so.

MR. CARTER: It didn't say go halfway down to Australia. You'll fall into it if you dig a pit like that. Now, are you all ready?

JENNINGS: Sir, can I run in my bare feet, sir?

MR. CARTER: No Jennings, you can't. What's the matter with your gym shoes?

JENNINGS: Well, sir, the book said we ought to have spiked shoes for running so I pushed some tin tacks through the soles of my gym shoes, but they keep working back inside and it's spivish lethal torture, sir, trying to run in them.

MR. CARTER: I'm sorry for you. Now, the course is one lap; follow the flags round behind the bowling-screen. On your marks... get set...

Starting pistol fired

HEADMASTER: Ah, there you are, Mr. Russell. I was just thinking how very fortunate you are to own a camera like that. I wish I had one.

MR. RUSSELL: Really? This is getting interesting.

HEADMASTER: It would be an invaluable acquisition. Think of the films we could take! Cricket, football, boxing, swimming, concerts, picnics, scouts. I'd give a lot for a cine like yours.

MR. RUSSELL: Seventy-five guineas?

HEADMASTER: I beg your pardon?

MR. RUSSELL: I'll sell you this one.

HEADMASTER: Oh, but that's yours; you need it yourself. I wouldn't dream of depriving you.

MR. RUSSELL: I can get another. You see, Headmaster, selling cameras happens to be my business.

HEADMASTER: Really? What a happy coincidence that you should think of coming to visit Jennings, today.

MR. RUSSELL: Er, - yes, quite a coincidence; must have been fate. Now, if you'll let me have a cheque for this camera, I'll show you how to use it.

HEADMASTER: Excellent! Just a moment, though, we must see the finish of this race; they're just rounding the bowling-screen. Venables is running third, Jennings is running second and... who's that boy in front? Good heavens, it's Darbishire! Run up, Darbishire! Faster, boy, faster! Jennings is gaining on him, rapidly, but Darbishire's lead is too great. He'll win if he sticks to it!... Quick, Mr. Russell, the camera! Darbishire winning a race is an event not to be missed. Here they come!

Fade in cheering and hold under

Darbishire first, Jennings second! Well run, Darbishire, I didn't think you had it in you!

DARBISHIRE: Thank you, sir, that's most awfully kind of you, sir. Mr. Carter told us to take it easy to start with, but I never really thought I'd win.

HEADMASTER: It's amazing, Mr. Carter; I never thought that boy would beat Jennings.

Fade out cheering

MR. CARTER: I think there's been a mistake, there, sir. Darbishire wasn't in that race.

HEADMASTER: But of course he was in it, Mr. Carter. He's just won it by a good three yards; I saw him.

MR. CARTER: No, sir, you didn't see Darbishire winning the 220; you saw him finishing a lap behind the others in the 440.

Fade to:

JENNINGS: Oh, Mr. Russell, sir, will you try and get a photo of Darbishire in the egg and spoon; you can't count him as being in the last race because they made him a displaced person.

HEADMASTER: Quick, Mr. Russell, the camera! Darbishire winning a race is an event not to be missed!

MR. RUSSELL: I'd love to, Jennings, but the Headmaster's got the camera now. He went rather higher than your bid of eleven and eightpence, so I sold it to him.

JENNINGS: Coo, wizzo. Bet he won't let us use it, though.

MR. RUSSELL: I should hope not. By the way, that Latin book you've got to pay for; how much is it?

JENNINGS: Five shillings, I think.

MR. RUSSELL: Well, here's ten.

JENNINGS: Oh, no, Mr. Russell, I couldn't possibly.

MR. RUSSELL: Of course you could. Call it your commission on the sale of the camera... Well, goodbye, I'm so glad to have met you; I don't know when I've enjoyed myself so much. I've had a wonderful day in the country, got you out of a hole and sold a camera. My manager will be pleased.

JENNINGS: Well, goodbye, Mr. Russell, it's been super having you and thanks for all you've done and everything.

MR. RUSSELL: I must just say goodbye to the Headmaster. Ah, there he is.

HEADMASTER: This camera's a most fascinating instrument, Mr. Russell. I happened to be taking a shot of Mr. Wilkins drinking a cup of tea, when Mr. Carter inadvertently let the starting-pistol off just behind him. And I now have a permanent photographic record in colour, of Mr. Wilkins' facial expression as he dropped the cup of tea on his trousers. Most diverting! Ha-ha-ha.

MR. RUSSELL: Well, goodbye, Headmaster.

HEADMASTER: Goodbye, Mr. Russell, and you'll remember me to the family next time you go to Haywards Heath, won't you?

MR. RUSSELL: Which family?

HEADMASTER: Mr. Jennings, of course.

MR. RUSSELL: Oh, er, yes, yes, of course. By the way, Headmaster, there's one small point that's been worrying my conscience for the last half hour.

HEADMASTER: Oh, what's that?

MR. RUSSELL: I suddenly remembered that the Mr. Jennings that I know lives at Weston-Super-Mare. Goodbye, (*fading*) I must hurry, or I'll miss that train.

HEADMASTER: Now, what on earth did he mean by... Jennings, come here.

JENNINGS: Yes, sir?

HEADMASTER: Didn't you tell me that Mr. Russell was a friend of your family?

JENNINGS: No, he said that, sir, I didn't.

HEADMASTER: But if he isn't, why on earth should he come down here specially to see you?

JENNINGS: Well, sir, you see, sir, it was like this, sir...

MR. CARTER: (*distant, through megaphone*) Egg and Spoon Race; Open.

JENNINGS: Oh, sir, this'll be a wonderful race for your camera, sir; it'll be super comic with everybody dropping their eggs.

HEADMASTER: I don't understand; I want to get this business of Mr. Russell straightened...

Starting pistol fired, distant

JENNINGS: Oo, sir, they're off, sir. Sir, do look at Darbishire, sir, his egg's wobbling like a... Quick, sir, your camera!

HEADMASTER: By jove, yes, I mustn't miss this. What do I do now? Ah yes, track in for a medium close shot... Move back, you boys there, you're standing right in my focus.

Whirr of cine camera, hold under:

JENNINGS: Isn't Darbishire funny, sir? He's dropped his egg and his glasses have come off, and he can't find his glasses to look for his egg!

HEADMASTER: Ha-ha-ha-, most diverting! I'm laughing so much I can't hold the camera steady. That's better, I've got an excellent picture of it now.

Stop whirr of cine camera

Well now, Jennings, I don't know who your friend Mr. Russell was, but I feel that the matter is of sufficient importance for me to take certain steps...

JENNINGS: (*desperately*) Oh, sir, please sir, really sir...

HEADMASTER: My considered opinion, therefore, is that if Mr. Russell is not a friend of the family... (*pauses*)

JENNINGS: (*gulping in apprehension*) Yes, sir?

HEADMASTER: If he is not already a friend of the family... then he most certainly ought to be.

JENNINGS
SEES THE LIGHT

(First series no.4)

Jennings Sees the Light was the fourth Jennings play.

It was first broadcast by the BBC Home Service for Children's Hour on 18th December 1948, with the following cast:

JENNINGS	David Page
DARBISHIRE	David Spenser
VENABLES	John Bishop
ATKINSON	John Cavanah
TEMPLE	Derek Rock
MR. CARTER	Geoffrey Wincott
MR. WILKINS	Wilfred Babbage
OLD NIGHTIE	David Kossoff

Fade in Morse buzzer tapping out a laborious S.O.S

DARBISHIRE: End of message; over to you, Jennings. Got it?

JENNINGS: Was the last one a dash or a dot?

DARBISHIRE: Three dots. Could you read it?

JENNINGS: I make it Big fig nop fos.

DARBISHIRE: Oh you are daft. That was S.O.S.

JENNINGS: What, again? That's the third time running you've done that one, Darbishire.

DARBISHIRE: It's the only one I can do without looking at the chart.

JENNINGS: Let me have a go. (*Morse buzzer taps out jumbled letters*) End of message. Got it Darbi?

DARBISHIRE: Yes. Merx pritzh ump thopshozz. Sounds like Polish to me.

JENNINGS: No, you fool. That was "My name is Jennings." Really Darbishire, if you're going to be my gang's wireless op. as well as intelligence officer, you'll have to do better than that.

DARBISHIRE: I'll be better when I've finished making the set. I'm going to get Mr. Carter to help me with the cat's whisker part.

JENNINGS: Wizzo. Then we'll be able to send out secret messages to America and aeroplanes and things.

DARBISHIRE: No we shan't. You can't make a transmitter with a crystal set. Still, it could be a secret receiving station if we don't tell anyone where it is.

JENNINGS: I vote we keep it behind the boot lockers when it's finished and make that my gang's headquarters. Will you be able to get short wave?

DARBISHIRE: Shouldn't think so. I might be able to get the Third programme though.

JENNINGS: Good. Then we can listen to Dick Barton and that other chap who misses death by inches in the jungle.

DARBISHIRE: But we're not allowed to listen to that.

JENNINGS: I know. That's why it's going to be a secret receiving station. Then one of us can fox out of prep, come down to the boot lockers and listen.

DARBISHIRE: Spivish rare. Temple's gang hasn't got a secret wireless.

JENNINGS: Neither have we yet. They'll have had time to make a crystal television set if you don't get a move on with your cat's whiskers. Come on, let's go down to headquarters.

Fade to:

DARBISHIRE: Dacka–dacka–dacka–dacka –

JENNINGS: Dacka-dacka-dacka-dacka – Got you Atkinson. Come on, you're a casualty.

ATKINSON: No I'm not, then, Jennings, 'cos this sweater's a bullet-proof waistcoat and it's not fair to shoot below the belt.

JENNINGS: That doesn't matter, you're standing on my tuck box and that's an unexploded minefield. Take him prisoner Intelligence Officer Darbishire.

DARBISHIRE: Okay Jennings, I mean Chief. Shall we put him up to ransom?

JENNINGS: Yes, the ransom price will be half a biscuit.

ATKINSON: Oh no, Jennings, that's not fair. No one would ever pay all that for me; make it an apple-core or something.

JENNINGS: I'll think about it. Meanwhile you'll stay here with Chief Intelligence Officer Darbishire.

DARBISHIRE: What if he escapes, Jennings?

JENNINGS: Warn all mobile patrols and shoot him within an inch of his life, I'm going on an air rescue in my plane.

DARBISHIRE: Righto. Goodbye, I mean happy landings.

JENNINGS: Eee-ow-eee-ow.

MR. CARTER: (*gasping*) Oh!

JENNINGS: I'm terribly sorry, sir. Really Mr. Carter, sir, I didn't mean to hit you...

MR. CARTER: Come here you clumsy little animal. Can't you go along this corridor without waving your arms and legs like a windmill? You can walk, I take it?

JENNINGS: Yes, sir.

MR. CARTER: This is the third time this week that your flailing
               tentacles have nearly knocked my teeth loose. On Monday
               you were practising imaginary leg breaks; yesterday you
               were a paddle-steamer on the Congo. What are you this
               time, a revolving door or a Catherine wheel?

JENNINGS: Neither, sir. I'm an autogyro.

MR. CARTER: H'm. Why is Atkinson tied to the clothes pegs?

JENNINGS: He's a prisoner, sir. You see, sir, he's in Temple's
               gang and we've captured him.

MR. CARTER: And what are all those bits of tin and similar junk?

JENNINGS: That's Darbishire's wireless set, sir. When it's built
               we'll be able to pick up messages from spies and
               underground resistances and things. You know, sir, like on
               the pictures. It'll be ever so exciting.

MR. CARTER: And what's that book on the floor there?

JENNINGS: It's the one I'm reading, sir. It's called "The Monster
               from Mars" and it's about a mad professor who invents a
               death ray and he nips into his rocket and beetles off to Mars
               and when he gets there...

MR. CARTER: Spare me the details. I've noticed for some time,
               Jennings, that your behaviour has been deteriorating and that
               your interests have become wild, lawless and unrestrained.
               Instead of walking about like a human being, you charge
               about mouthing mechanical engine noises; the energy you
               should be devoting to organised games is being wasted in
               ridiculous gang warfare, and instead of using the library
               intelligently and developing a taste for worthwhile literature,
               I find you wallowing in ill-written blood and thunder. Give
               me that book.

JENNINGS: It's not all thud and blunder, sir, there's quite a lot
               about science and stuff.

MR. CARTER: Give it to me and in future I want to see all your books
               before you read them. I'll confiscate the wireless too.
               Furthermore, the gangs will be disbanded at once and there's
               to be no more gang games.

JENNINGS: Oh, sir!

MR. CARTER: Definitely not. You're getting too old, Jennings, for
               all this rowdy puerile hooliganism. It's time you learnt
               discrimination and developed a sense of the fitness of things.

JENNINGS: Yes, sir.

Fade to:

DARBISHIRE: It's a rotten shame about my crystal set.

JENNINGS: That's the trouble with masters; they don't appreciate anything intelligent. I mean, we could have listened to symphony concerts and talks on economics and things couldn't we?

DARBISHIRE: Yes, of course we could. And just switched over to the other programme when there was nothing else specially highbrow to listen to. We shan't be allowed to do anything soon, without permission. Won't it sound cuckoo saying "Please, sir, may I breathe?"

JENNINGS: Might as well be in a concentration camp. I think Mr. Carter's a spivish oik and a putrid dago.

DARBISHIRE: I thought you liked him?

JENNINGS: Of course I do, I like him better than any other grown-up I know; except my father.

DARBISHIRE: How can he be a rotter, then?

JENNINGS: Well, surely you can call your best friend names if you want to? It's a free country.

DARBISHIRE: Well, what can we do now we can't play gangs?

JENNINGS: As a matter of fact, I've got a rather prang idea. You know that cottage the far side of the quad that Matron uses for a sanitorium? Well, I can see it from my window in the dorm.

DARBISHIRE: So can I; there's nothing very spivish about that.

JENNINGS: No, but several times this term when I've woken up in the night, I've looked out of the window and what d'you think I've seen?

DARBISHIRE: Mr. Carter and the Head dancing in the moonlight.

JENNINGS: Don't be so wet. No; I've seen a light in the san.

DARBISHIRE: What of it? It only means Matron's forgotten to turn it off.

JENNINGS: But don't you see, Darbishire, no one's used the san this term. We haven't had a measle or a mump for donkey's years. The cottage is supposed to be empty.

DARBISHIRE: Crumbs! Who d'you think's there then? Spies or forgers or what?

JENNINGS: Burglars I expect. They know no one goes over there, so they've probably been burgling the place night after night and nobody knows. It must be nearly empty by now if I'm right.

DARBISHIRE: What shall we do; tell Mr. Carter?

JENNINGS: No, that'd spoil it. But next time I see the light it'd be a wizard prang if we went over there and spied on them red-handed; then we could beetle off to that phone box at the end of the drive and dial 999.

DARBISHIRE: Rather! Witch prang!

JENNINGS: What do you mean, "which prang"? There is only one.

DARBISHIRE: No, I didn't mean "which" prang, I meant "witch" prang. W.I.T.C.H. Witch. You know, black cats and flying on broomsticks.

JENNINGS: Who's flying on broomsticks?

DARBISHIRE: Witches do.

JENNINGS: What about it?

DARBISHIRE: Nothing – when you told me your idea I just said "witch prang". It's the feminine of Wizard prang. Witch Prang is Wizard Prang's wife.

JENNINGS: How'd you know?

DARBISHIRE: I made up a story about them in bed the other night. The neighbours don't know they can work spells and they just think they're Mr. and Mrs. W. Prang of "Chez Nous" and they've got a son called Goblin Prang Esquire who works in the Post Office... yes, and Witch Prang is very up to date and flies on a vacuum cleaner and instead of a cauldron she's got a thermostic controlled electric dishwasher and...

JENNINGS: Oh you're crackers, Darbishire. Don't you want to hear about my wheeze?

DARBISHIRE: Of course I do, but just now you called it a prang and I said...

JENNINGS: All right, all right. Now, I vote that one of us wakes up about twelve o'clock and wakes the other one and then we get hockey sticks in case we're attacked and we could let ourselves out of the window on the Davey fire escape.

DARBISHIRE: Wouldn't it be easier just to walk down the stairs?

JENNINGS: I s'pose it would really, I never thought of that. Anyway, we'd better let Venables or someone know in case we don't come back, and when it's twelve o'clock we...

DARBISHIRE: Yes, but how's one of us going to wake up at twelve o'clock?

JENNINGS: Well, if we had an alarm clock we could set it for twelve o'clock and then fix it to my ear by tying my braces round my head.

DARBISHIRE: Coo yes, super-duper... But s'pose you turned over in your sleep; you might bust the glass.

JENNINGS: I thought of that. When I've tied it on I'll get into bed and lie on my side and you tie my hands to the bedpost with my tie so's I can't turn over.

DARBISHIRE: That'd be smashing... Yes, but if your hands are tied to the bed rail, how are you going to switch the alarm off?

JENNINGS: Oh! Well how'd it be if, when it went off, I called out to you and woke you up, then you could nip out of bed and untie my hands and I could switch the alarm off.

DARBISHIRE: It might have run down by then, I'm rather a heavy sleeper.

JENNINGS: Well you'd have to wake up for the scheme to work, 'cos I won't be able to get out of bed till you've undone my hands.

DARBISHIRE: All right then, Jennings, let's do that. It'll be a smash on priority prang.

JENNINGS: There's just one snag though.

DARBISHIRE: What?

JENNINGS: We haven't got an alarm clock.

DARBISHIRE: Oh... That's rather a bore, isn't it?

JENNINGS: We'll just have to keep awake, that's all. And we must write a note in case things go wrong, so's we can be rescued.

DARBISHIRE: Oh golly. Is it going to be hefty dangerous?

JENNINGS: P'raps, but not lethal. You see, everything's all right 'cos the note tells them where you've gone and then they surround the place with flying squads and things. I read a book about a chap who was going to another chap's house and he didn't trust this chap, the first one didn't, so the first chap gave a note to his butler and if he hadn't come back

87

from this chap's house by next morning, he was to take it to Scotland yard. And when the chap got to the other chap's house, he was jolly glad he had, the first chap I mean, not the chap whose house he was going to...

DARBISHIRE: Yes, but what's the good of telling me all this? We haven't got a butler. First we hadn't got an alarm clock and now we haven't got...

JENNINGS: But you don't have to have a butler.

DARBISHIRE: You said we did.

JENNINGS: I said that's what the chap did. The first chap I mean, not the chap whose house...

DARBISHIRE: All right, I know. Look, there's Venables, couldn't we just tell him instead of leaving a note?

JENNINGS: Okay. Venables, come here!

VENABLES: What d'you want, Jennings?

JENNINGS: Will you do me a favour?

VENABLES: If you mean will I swap you my ten cent Liberian three-cornered stamp...

JENNINGS: No, it's not that.

VENABLES: And I'm not going to lend you my...

JENNINGS: Not that sort of a favour. Listen, I've got a top priority urgent secret. Can I trust you?

VENABLES: Yes, of course. I won't breathe a word.

JENNINGS: Swear?

VENABLES: Yes, rather, what is it?

JENNINGS: Well, I've seen lights in the san and Darbi and I are going over in the middle of the night to investigate 'cos we think it's burglars and if we don't come back...

Fade out. Pause. Fade in:

VENABLES: I say, Atkinson.

ATKINSON: Oh, buzz off, Venables; can't you see I'm busy?

VENABLES: All right, then, but I know something that's a top priority hush, like invasion plans and things.

ATKINSON: Oh, tell me; go on, be decent.

VENABLES: 'Fraid I can't; it's lethal confidential.

ATKINSON: Look, if you tell me, I'll put you on my Cake List.

VENABLES: But you said you'd done that weeks ago.

ATKINSON: Well, if you don't tell me, I'll cross you off.

VENABLES: All right, then, but you mustn't split.

ATKINSON: Okay.

VENABLES: Well, Jen and Darbi are going over to the san at midnight, 'cos they think it's burglars, but I think it's probably spies who've landed on the beach and they're after the Government's secret plans.

ATKINSON: What secret plans?

VENABLES: No special ones, - just secret plans; there's bound to be masses of secret plans about...

Fade to:

ATKINSON: I say, Temple, I've heard something; it's hairy daring!

TEMPLE: I s'pose you've been earwigging again, Atkinson?

ATKINSON: No I haven't, honestly.

TEMPLE: You always did have supersonic earsight.

ATKINSON: No, really; Jennings has seen lights in the san and Venables thinks it's spies, but I think it's black marketeers and they've probably got the place crammed from floor to ceiling with rare valuables; you know, four-bladed pen-knives and model yachts and rare stamps and things you can't get, like chewing gum and sweets with four flavours, - you know, really important stuff...

Fade to:

TEMPLE: I say, Venables, have you heard about the lights in the san?

VENABLES: That's hairy stale buns; I was the first to know. I'd like to know how you found out, it's s'posed to be corking secret, but if it gets round like this we might as well have it broadcast on the six o'clock news. Jennings told me about it 'cos I was the only one he could trust. And now everyone knows, it's a bit thick the way chaps can't keep their mouths shut.

TEMPLE: Who's told everyone; you have.

VENABLES: I only told Atkinson; he isn't everybody.

TEMPLE: I think it's a spivish rotten secret. The only people who don't know now are the masters and if you go on like this...

Fade. Door knock

MR. CARTER: Come in.

Door opens:

Oh hullo Wilkins.

MR. WILKINS: Look here, Carter, I've discovered something you ought to know – Jennings and Darbishire have spotted lights in the san late at night.

MR. CARTER: Yes, I know.

MR. WILKINS: You know?

MR. CARTER: Everybody knows by now, don't they?

MR. WILKINS: Probably. I heard two of them behind the boot lockers whispering away at the tops of their voices. Who told you?

MR. CARTER: I'm afraid I couldn't help overhearing either. Jennings has got a whisper like a loud-hailer, especially when he's relating a particularly confidential secret.

MR. WILKINS: Exactly. And I'll tell you another thing. They're planning to go over there at night and investigate.

MR. CARTER: Yes, I know that too.

MR. WILKINS: What are you going to do about it?

MR. CARTER: I shan't stop them.

MR. WILKINS: You won't...? But good heavens, Carter, this is serious. If tramps are using the san to sleep in, it's a police matter.

MR. CARTER: I don't think we'll bother the police just yet.

MR. WILKINS: But don't you realise that these two silly little boys are planning to go there? They might easily get knocked on the head. Did you think of that? Now are you going to stop them?

MR. CARTER: No.

MR. WILKINS: In heaven's name, why?

MR. CARTER: It's like this, Wilkins. Jennings has been getting very wild lately, and so far my efforts to turn him into a respectable member of society haven't worked. I got them interested in building a crystal set only to find that their real aim was to listen to programmes during prep. I had to take Jennings off detective stories after that embarrassing scene when he deduced that the new kitchen man was an escaped convict by the way he tied his bootlaces.

MR. WILKINS: Heavens, yes; we had an awful time pacifying the maids and apologising all round, didn't we?

MR. CARTER: Today, I put a stop to his playing gangs and half an hour later, here he is hatching another piece of excitement.

MR. WILKINS: Put your foot down, then. Stop it at once.

MR. CARTER: I'm trying to point out to you that when I nip these enterprises in the bud, they crop up again elsewhere. If I stop this sanitorium expedition, he'll have thought up something else by tomorrow.

MR. WILKINS: But you can't let them walk into danger like that. They don't realise...

MR. CARTER: If we let them go this time, they certainly won't enjoy it, it'll kerb their taste for adventure much more effectively than saying, "thou shalt not".

MR. WILKINS: But what about the tramps? They won't knock them on the head gently just to kerb their taste for adventure.

MR. CARTER: Wilkins, you jump to conclusions just as Jennings does. What makes you think there are tramps in the san?

MR. WILKINS: The lights, of course; when it's empty.

MR. CARTER: Those lights are on every night between ten and eleven o'clock, because that's the time that Old Nightie cleans the place.

MR. WILKINS: Old Nightie? You mean the night-watchman? Oh, I see, that explains the lights.

MR. CARTER: Yes, but if I tell Jennings that, he'll be on the hunt for some new scheme; so I've decided what to do. I shall tell Old Nightie that two boys may interrupt his labours one evening when he's sweeping up. If they do, he's to take hold of them gently but firmly and lock them in one of the rooms. Then he can come and tell me. It's all perfectly safe; I'll allow a little while for the excitement to evaporate and it should be a somewhat chastened Jennings and Darbishire who get led back to bed when their firework turns out to be a damp squib.

MR. WILKINS: By jove, yes! That'll cool their hot heads for them.

MR. CARTER: Come along then; we'll go and find Old Nightie and tell him what to expect.

Fade out. Pause. Fade in:

JENNINGS: *(whispering)* Darbishire!   Wake up!   Wake up, Darbishire!

DARBISHIRE: Uh?

JENNINGS: Wake up, man; it's urgent.

DARBISHIRE: Wassmarrer?

JENNINGS: It's me; Jennings. Listen, are you awake, Darbi?

DARBISHIRE: I'm not sure; I think so.

JENNINGS: Well, listen; I've seen the light.

DARBISHIRE: Have you? Oh good, I'm so glad. I heard a man at a missionary jumble sale who said he'd seen the light. Up to that time he'd been a notorious...

JENNINGS: Listen, Darbi; it's the burglar.

DARBISHIRE: I don't think he was a burglar. He said he was a brand plucked from the burning.

JENNINGS: Who said?

DARBISHIRE: The notorious evil-doer at the missionary jumble sale who saw the light.

JENNINGS: Oh, wake up and talk sense. There's a burglar in the san.

DARBISHIRE: How d'you know?

JENNINGS: I've told you. I've just seen the... well, there's a light burning.

DARBISHIRE: Oh golly, yes of course. I remember now.

JENNINGS: Come on then; we're going over there.

DARBISHIRE: Oh!... Er, - me too?

JENNINGS: You said you would.

DARBISHIRE: Well it seemed rather a hairy prang this afternoon, but I don't think I'll bother now, if you don't mind.

JENNINGS: Don't be a funk, Darbi. You're not frightened are you?

DARBISHIRE: Well,... my father says that discretion is the better part of...

JENNINGS: All the chaps said you'd be frightened. Here's your chance to prove they're wrong.

DARBISHIRE: I can't prove them wrong, 'cos I'll still be frightened even if I go.

JENNINGS: It's quite safe. We'll just have a dekko to make sure it's burglars and then we'll phone the police.

DARBISHIRE: Well, no dacka-dacka-dacka stuff and taking prisoners like those gang games.

JENNINGS: Of course not; this is the real thing.

DARBISHIRE: I know, that's the trouble; you can't say pax when you've had enough.

JENNINGS: Look, here's a hockey stick for you; put your dressing gown on and creep out quietly.

Pause. Fade in footsteps and hold under:

DARBISHIRE: Can't we go back, Jen?

JENNINGS: Lord, no; don't be such a funk, Darbishire.

DARBISHIRE: Oh no, don't think I'm frightened - much.

JENNINGS: Why talk about going back then?

DARBISHIRE: Well, er, I've got a sore place on my heel and Matron said not to walk on it too much.

JENNINGS: But if we go back we'll miss all the excitement.

DARBISHIRE: Well, we could still talk about it and after all these things are much more fun to talk about than they are to do.

JENNINGS: Come on, we'll be there in a minute. Look, you can see the light plainly.

DARBISHIRE: I feel like that chap in a poem *who on a lonesome road doth walk in fear and dread...*

JENNINGS: I think I can see his shadow moving on the curtain upstairs.

DARBISHIRE: *And having once looked back, walks on and turns no more his head.*

JENNINGS: We mustn't let him see us; we'll have to creep in like mice.

DARBISHIRE: *Because he knows a frightful fiend doth close behind him tread.*

JENNINGS: What are you nattering about?

DARBISHIRE: I said "a frightful fiend doth close behind him tread".

JENNINGS: Treads close behind who?

DARBISHIRE: Anyone who on a lonesome road doth walk...

JENNINGS: I can't see anyone.

DARBISHIRE: Of course you can't; there's no one there.

JENNINGS: You said there was.

DARBISHIRE: I said the chap in the poem thought there was, so having once looked back...

JENNINGS: You're goofy, Darbishire. Here we are in the middle of an adventure and you start reciting poetry.

Stop footsteps

Look, the french window's open; I shan't have to use my skeleton key after all.

DARBISHIRE: Have you got one?

JENNINGS: It's my tuck-box key, really, but it fits the stationery cupboard, so it'll probably open anything. Come on..! Sh! We'll go through into the hall. I'll hold my hockey stick at the ready and you open the door quietly. Sh! Sh!

Door opens. Jennings gasps

JENNINGS: Oooh!

DARBISHIRE: W-w-what's the matter?

JENNINGS: Sh! It's all right. I thought I saw someone coming at me with a club, but it's my reflection in that mirror over there. Sh! We'll go upstairs. Sh!

DARBISHIRE: D-d-don't keep saying Sh! It m-makes more r-row than not sh-shushing at all.

Pause. Footsteps on stairs

JENNINGS: He's in that bedroom there; I can hear him. Sounds as though he's moving furniture about.

DARBISHIRE: C-come on, let's g-go then. We've got to ph-phone the police.

JENNINGS: Come on then; let's go down again quietly. Can't you stop your teeth chattering?

DARBISHIRE: I've got the w-wind up, that's why. My heart's beating like a s-s-sledge hammer.

Hockey stick falls down stairs, bumping on each stair as it goes

Oh gosh, I've dropped my hockey stick.

JENNINGS: He'll hear it; oh golly, what shall we do now?

Door opens violently

DARBISHIRE: Oh gosh, the bur-bur-burglar!

GRUFF VOICE: What you doing 'ere?

JENNINGS: N-nothing.

DARBISHIRE: I feel like that chap in a poem who on a lonesome road
doth walk in fear and dread…
*JENNINGS: You're goofy, Darbishire. Here we are in the middle of an
adventure and you start reciting poetry.*

GRUFF VOICE: Wotcher mean, nuffing?

JENNINGS: Nothing, thank you very much.

GRUFF VOICE: 'Ere you, get in that room there, both on yer; and you keep quiet till I'm gorn or you'll cop it.

JENNINGS: No, no, let go of me. Darbi, call for help.

DARBISHIRE: (*voiceless with fright*) H-h-h-help!

JENNINGS: Take your hands off me. Let me alone!

Sounds of pushing and scuffling

GRUFF VOICE: Go in there and keep yer mouths shut.

Door slams. Key turns in lock

DARBISHIRE: Oh!…Oh!…Oh golly!

JENNINGS: (*gasping*) Are you all right, Darbi?

DARBISHIRE: I think so. He… He's locked us in, hasn't he?

Door handle rattles

JENNINGS: Yes, and we're on the first floor, so we can't get out of the window.

DARBISHIRE: How about shouting for help?

JENNINGS: They'd never hear us; it's too far.

DARBISHIRE: What's going to happen, then?

JENNINGS: He's locked us in so's he can make a getaway; if only we could stop him.

DARBISHIRE: I don't want to stop him. The further the getaway the better.

JENNINGS: Let's put the light on and see where we are.

Click of light switch

We're in the night nurse's sitting-room. Look, Darbi, over there!

DARBISHIRE: I can't s-see anything; my teeth are chattering too much.

JENNINGS: You don't see with your teeth, do you?

DARBISHIRE: No, but I'm trembling such a lot I can't put my glasses on. What is it?

JENNINGS: It's a telephone. Gosh, that's lucky; we can phone the police from here. I wonder what the number is.

DARBISHIRE: You just say Police or Fire or Ambulance, whichever you want. Look , I vote we ask for the ambulance as well in case we see that man again.

JENNINGS: There's a sort of handle thing at the side. I s'pose you have to turn it round.

Telephone generator handle turned.

Fade to telephone bell ringing and continue intermittently

MR. WILKINS: Shall I answer the phone, Carter?

MR. CARTER: Thank you, Wilkins. I can't think who can be... here, wait a minute; that's not an exchange call: it's switched over to the extension.

MR. WILKINS: What of it? It's probably the Headmaster.

MR. CARTER: It couldn't be on that line; that's through to the sanitorium. I expect it's Old Nightie ringing up to say he's done his bit of dirty work and locked them in.

MR. WILKINS: They have gone, then?

MR. CARTER: Oh yes. I heard the patter of little feet past my door just before you came in; only their tip-toeing sounded more like a cavalry regiment thundering across the plain.

MR. WILKINS: I'd better see what Old Nightie's got to say.

Telephone receiver lifted from hook

Hullo?... Put you through to the...? Er, all right; wait a minute. (*Whispering*) It's Jennings. He thinks I'm the exchange and he wants the Police Station. It's no good, Carter; I can't resist the temptation; I've always wanted to be a policeman. (*Stops whispering and assumes heavily disguised voice*) Hullo?... Yes, Police Station here. Sergeant Snackbar speaking... What? A burglar? H'm; you're sure he's a burglar and not a spy or a foreigner or a black-marketeer?... I see. Locked you in eh, tut tut, tut tut, that's bad. The larks these burglars get up to!... What's that? You want me to catch him?... Yes, but if I come round to a sanitorium I'm more likely to catch measles than burglars... Then what's he doing in a sanitorium if he's not ill?... Ah, maybe he wasn't when he first broke in, but he's bound to be infectious by now... Well, all right. I'll send a couple of flying-squads round as soon as they've finished their supper. Goodbye.

Receiver replaced

Ha-ha-ha-ha! Oh dear, oh dear, that was funny! Old Nightie's locked them in and they're not enjoying it. I think it's cooled their hot heads all right.

MR. CARTER: Come along, let's go and let them out. They ought to be cured of their taste for adventure by now.

Door opens. Footsteps in corridor. Hold under:

MR. WILKINS: There's Old Nightie, look! He's coming to tell us what's happened.

MR. CARTER: Good evening, Hawkins.

OLD NIGHTIE: 'Evening, Mr. Carter, sir.

MR. CARTER: I gather you've got the boys safely in your care.

OLD NIGHTIE: Eh? No, not yet I 'aven't. I ain't been over to the sanitorium yet. I'm just a-going now.

MR. WILKINS: What!!

MR. CARTER: You've not been over there yet?

OLD NIGHTIE: No, sir. Got 'eld up with the clinker in the boiler down the stoke 'ole. First time I bin late for cleaning the san these four years. Ten o'clock, reg'lar as clockwork, bar tonight.

MR. WILKINS: But if you haven't been over there...

OLD NIGHTIE: It's all right, Mr. Wilkins, I'm going now. I'll get finished there by ar past eleven and if it 'adn't bin for the clinker in the boiler...

MR. CARTER: I don't understand this. Wilkins, didn't Jennings tell you he'd been locked in a room?

MR. WILKINS: Yes, he said they'd met a burglar. I took it for granted it was Old Nightie, - I beg your pardon, Hawkins, I mean I thought it was you.

OLD NIGHTIE: Couldn't very well 'ave been me, could it, seeing as how I was down the stoke 'ole getting the clinker out of the...

MR. CARTER: Come on, let's get over there quickly. I don't like this.

Running footsteps. Dialogue interspersed with panting

Really, Wilkins. I think you might have found out what was going on over there instead of assing about on the phone like that.

MR. WILKINS: I thought my little effort was rather good.

MR. CARTER: Sergeant Snackbar indeed! What nonsense you talk!

MR. WILKINS: Didn't it sound convincing? I was rather proud of it.

MR. CARTER: You sounded like a comic pantomime cop.

MR. WILKINS: I say, Carter, that's a bit harsh. I hoped you'd think it was like Robb Wilton. Anyway, you're a nice one to talk! Who let them go over there in the first place?

MR. CARTER: I know all about that; that's what's worrying me. Can't you run any faster?

MR. WILKINS: (*panting harder*) Give me a chance, old man; I'm forty six round the middle.

OLD NIGHTIE: (*panting*) Wot's all the 'urry about, Mr. Carter? Is there anything wrong?

MR. CARTER: That's what I'm going to find out... Wait! Look, over there by the hedge! I can see something moving.

Slow footsteps down

OLD NIGHTIE: One o' them cats, most like.

MR. CARTER: That's not a cat; it's got two legs and a kit bag. After him, quick!

Bring up running footsteps

He's seen us; he's running away; come on... round the other way and we'll catch him... here he is; we've got him!

Noise of scuffling, panting and dull thuds

MR. WILKINS: Got him, Carter?

MR. CARTER: Yes... Come on, up you get. We'll put him in this coal cellar; have you got a key for it Hawkins?

OLD NIGHTIE: Yes, sir, it's 'ere on me key ring.

Key turns in lock:

Well, a burglar in the san on the one night in four years I bin late on the job! What do you know about that? If it 'adn't been for that bit o' clinker in the boiler...

MR. WILKINS: What's he got in the kit bag, Nightie?

OLD NIGHTIE: Nothing much, sir. An 'ot water bottle, an ear-syringe, the old clock wot don't go, two packets o' cotton wool, about 'alf a mile o' bandages and a bottle o' castor oil. Some people ain't got no sense; now if he'd broke into the libery he could 'ave pinched all them silver cups.

MR. CARTER: Come on, Wilkins, I'm going to see if those boys are all right.

Fade in shouts distant and bring up:

JENNINGS: Help! Help! Rescue!

DARBISHIRE: HELP! Help! Burglars! Police!

MR. CARTER: They sound lively enough, anyway. Come along let's go in; the french windows are open... Oh, come along, Wilkins, upstairs, quick!

MR. WILKINS: (*gasping*) There's no hurry now, is there? I've done the last hundred yards in a good two seconds under the European record.

MR. CARTER: (*calling*) Jennings, where are you?

JENNINGS: In here, sir!

Door handle tried

MR. CARTER: It's locked; we'll have to force it. Here, Wilkins, try your thirteen stone on the door.

MR. WILKINS: Righto, stand back!

Door crashes open

JENNINGS: Oh sir, I'm ever so glad you heard us, sir, there's been a burglar, sir.

MR. CARTER: Yes I know; we've got him.

JENNINGS: Oh, wizzo!

MR. CARTER: Are you all right, Jennings?

JENNINGS: Yes, sir.

MR. CARTER: And you, Darbishire?

DARBISHIRE: I'm just a bit shaken up, sir, but I'm very well, thank you, considering.

MR. CARTER: Thank goodness for that. I was very worried about you.

JENNINGS: I shouldn't be surprised if we weren't both suffering from shock, sir. Don't you think it would be a good thing if we were to take things quietly in class for the next few days, sir?

MR. WILKINS: It'd be a change, anyway, to have you quiet in class.

JENNINGS: I mean not overdo things by working too hard and straining ourselves, sir.

MR. WILKINS: That would *not* be a change.

MR. CARTER: If you're all right, you'd better be getting back to bed. I shall have to phone the police about this burglar chap.

JENNINGS: I've done that already, sir; they're sending two flying-squads. I can't think why they're not here already.

MR. CARTER: I can. Can't you, Mr. Wilkins?

JENNINGS: The sergeant said he'd see to it, but he sounded a very stupid sort of man, sir.

MR. CARTER: Really, now, that's very interesting! Stupid, you said.

JENNINGS: Yes, sir, he'd got no sense; he seemed to think it was funny.

MR. CARTER: Fancy! What do you make of that Mr. Wilkins?

MR. WILKINS: All right, all right. You don't have to keep on about it.

JENNINGS: But sir, it's spivish about Darbishire and me catching the burglar, isn't it, sir? He'd have got away with thousands of pounds of stuff, p'raps. Will there be a reward, sir, and will I have to go and be a witness?

MR. CARTER: Not if I know it. Look here, Jennings, you've had quite enough excitement for one evening.

JENNINGS: Yes sir, but it'll be hairy latest news when the other chaps hear about it, 'cos they said Darbishire would be afraid and he wasn't, was he sir, were you Darbi?

DARBISHIRE: My father says that courage in adversity is a quality which can only be…

JENNINGS: Oh sir, they'll all be as sick as mud when they know what they've slept through. Oh, smash on, I'm going to have a galumphing delectable time tomorrow.

Fade out. Pause. Fade in:

MR. CARTER: You know, Wilkins, I'm afraid I've come out of this rather badly. With things turning out as they did, I hadn't the heart to take them down a peg.

MR. WILKINS: That's what comes of trying to be clever; I'm afraid your little scheme to cure them's going to have just the opposite effect.

MR. CARTER: You've no cause to be exuberant about it, either. It ought to be a long time before you imitate any more policemen. Still, it was just bad luck they chose the one night there happened to be a real burglar.

MR. WILKINS: I was forgetting about him; have you phoned the police yet?

MR. CARTER: No, I told Old Nightie to let him go.

MR. WILKINS: Let him go! Whatever for?

MR. CARTER: Jennings will get enough glory out of this without having to give evidence in court. And if I'm going to make him into a civilised human being, it's obvious I shall have to try other methods.

MR. WILKINS: What are you going to do then?

MR. CARTER: I don't know yet, but I can tell you one thing. The next time I get to work on him, there won't be a Police-Sergeant Snackbar in the cast. I'm going round the dormitory now; I want to make sure they've gone to sleep.

Fade to soft footsteps.

The remaining dialogue is spoken in whispered tones

MR. CARTER: Are you asleep yet, Jennings?

JENNINGS: No, sir, I'm much too excited. Darbishire is though, sir. He was just telling me what his father always says about something and he dropped off in the middle… Sir, will you come and sit down on my bed, sir, please? I don't feel like going to sleep; I want to talk about the burglary.

MR. CARTER: Oh, Jennings, whatever am I going to make of you? The harder I try, the worse you get.

JENNINGS: Well, sir, I was thinking, sir, you know you stopped us playing gangs because it was too rowdy?

MR. CARTER: I do.

JENNINGS: Well sir, wouldn't it be quieter if we played burglaries instead? You see, Venables or someone could be the burglar and Atkinson could be locked in a room like we were, only it would have to be behind the boot lockers, really, and Darbishire could be the telephone exchange with his Morse buzzer and I'd be the Chief of the flying-squad, and when I got the message I'd nip into my autogyro…

MR. CARTER: And rush round the corridors with your arms rotating like a roundabout and knock my pipe out of my mouth; I know. Why can't you play something quiet; like chess?

JENNINGS: Well, we could bring that in too, sir. We could give Venables, or whoever the burglar was, twenty years in prison and when Darbishire'd finished being the telephone exchange, he could be a warder and go and play chess with the lonely convict…

Start slow fade:

…to cheer him up a bit in his cell, only it'd have to be behind the boot lockers, really, and we could pretend…

Fade out.

JENNINGS
AND THE VERY IMPORTANT PARENT

(First series no.5)

Jennings and the Very Important Parent was the fifth Jennings play.

It was first broadcast by the BBC Home Service for Children's Hour on 15th January 1949, with the following cast:

JENNINGS	David Page
DARBISHIRE	Loris Somerville
TEMPLE	David Spenser
VENABLES	John Bishop
MR. CARTER	Geoffrey Wincott
THE HEADMASTER	Laidman Browne
LORD FALCONBRIDGE	Bruce Belfrage
TALBOT FALCONBRIDGE	Julian Belfrage

Fade in sound of hammering

JENNINGS: Don't make such a row, Darbishire.

DARBISHIRE: Well, I can't knock nails in quietly, can I?

JENNINGS: You can if you want to. Why don't you hammer with your shoe instead of your pencil box?

DARBISHIRE: It's all very well for you, Jennings; your shoes have got rubber heels, but mine have got sort of iron horse-shoe things and it'd make sparks and p'raps set the hut on fire.

JENNINGS: Well, I can't lend you my other shoe, 'cos I've got to stand on one leg as it is with all these puddles and mud all over the floor.

DARBISHIRE: Never mind; it's beginning to look quite like a hut, isn't it? I vote we show Temple and Venables; they'll be as sick as coots when they see it. Their hut isn't nearly as good as this.

JENNINGS: Okay. (*Calling*) Venables! Bod! Come and see how we're getting on... I bet they haven't got a secret spy hole in their hut.

DARBISHIRE: Neither would we if you hadn't stuck your elbow through my prefabricated ventilation shaft... Hello, Bod; like to see our hut?

TEMPLE: H'm. It's not bad, Darbishire, considering you and Jennings made it.

JENNINGS: I'll show you round. This is the front door and it's the dining table as well. That's one of Darbishire's inventions.

DARBISHIRE: And it can also be used as duck boards when the floor's muddy; like this, Venables, look. It's spivish delectable.

VENABLES: I don't know about duck boards; you'll need stilts if it gets any wetter.

DARBISHIRE: Ah, but that's all right, 'cos I've invented a famous special irrigation canal to drain the floor when it rains and it's a super decent thing to have masses of water, 'cos we could withstand a siege for months and months if we got beleaguered. Why, we could wash if we felt like it.

TEMPLE: I can't see either you or Jennings going quite as far as that. What's that old petrol tin for, Jennings?

106

JENNINGS: When it's full, it's either emergency drinking supply or a patent fire extinguisher, and when it's empty, it's a tribal tom-tom for beating out messages. Or, if you like, you can have a little light drum music to lull you to sleep. Like this.

Banging on petrol can

TEMPLE: Coo, smashing! What's in there?

JENNINGS: That's the air-conditioned larder. We've got a pork pie we've been saving up for ages so's we can have a banquet when we get next month's sweet rations.

DARBISHIRE: I don't think we ought to wait till then, Jennings. That sort of cotton wool stuff's spreading all over it like anything, in spite of air-conditioning.

JENNINGS: Oh, I don't suppose it'll taste much if we scrape it off.

TEMPLE: And what's through that hole, there?

JENNINGS: That's the small back room.

VENABLES: Why ever d'you want two rooms? Our hut's only got one.

JENNINGS: Ah, but we have to have the small back room, 'cos Darbishire's been appointed chief boffin.

DARBISHIRE: Yes, I'm the back-room boy and I go in there and invent things. Hefty intricate, some of them. I'm working on a rare patent doormat, now, with "Welcome to ye olde worlde hutte" picked out in coloured fizzy drink bottle tops.

TEMPLE: Why can't you just say, "old world hut"?

DARBISHIRE: Oh no, you have to put "e"s on the end of words, 'cos that's how they spelt it in the Stone Age.

JENNINGS: That's right; so you see, we've got to have a small back room to keep the boffin in.

DARBISHIRE: Yes, and here's another brainy prang I dashed off yesterday; it's a mammoth how-many-more-days-till-we-break-up calendar.

VENABLES: That's not your invention; we all make those the last week of term.

DARBISHIRE: Yes, but with mine, you start crossing off the days from the beginning of term; and it's got other useful data too. F'rinstance, from now, there's seventy three more days before we go home, or one thousand, seven hundred and fifty-two hours and sixty-seven more Latin lessons and seventy-one Maths, including mental arith'; corned beef for

107

lunch thirty-three times, that ozard gluey pudding muck twenty-one times, and date cake eleven; so you see it's all spivish convenient information to know.

TEMPLE: You'd better not let Mr. Carter see you've got that chisel; it belongs to the carpenter's shop.

JENNINGS: I don't think he'd mind our borrowing it, he's smashing decent, really.

VENABLES: Yes, it's not often you find grown-ups who think huts are wizard.

JENNINGS: They seem to turn against things like that when they get old.

TEMPLE: Mr. Carter's not old, Jennings.

JENNINGS: Oh, he is. I bet he's twenty anyway; more than that, probably; say, forty-five or fifty.

DARBISHIRE: He must be fairly ancient, 'cos he was alive in the olden days.

TEMPLE: He ought to be able to read your olde worlde hutte language, then.

DARBISHIRE: Oh, not all that old, of course, but he can remember right back to before they'd invented things like jet-propelled for aeroplanes and coupons for sweets. Why, when he was young, I don't suppose they'd ever heard of railways, trains and identity cards and things.

JENNINGS: Come on, let's go outside and I'll show you our bridge that Darbi and I are building over the swampy part.

DARBISHIRE: I'm rather proud of this bridge, actually. It incorporates the more smashing features of the Bailey bridge except that we've used football bootlaces tied in clove hitches instead of... oh golly, here's the Head coming. Cave.

TEMPLE: That's all right, Mr. Carter said we could come over here.

JENNINGS: Yes, but all the same, I can't see why the Head should be so interested in...

OMNES: Good afternoon, sir.

HEADMASTER: Good afternoon. So these are the huts I've heard such a lot about, are they?

OMNES: Yes, sir.

HEADMASTER: If you must build huts, I can't think why you have to choose the muddiest corner of the playing-fields next to the pond. Neither can I understand why Jennings should be standing in a puddle with only one shoe on.

JENNINGS: I'm sorry, sir, I've been using the other one for a - er, I mean, I hardly noticed the puddle, sir.

HEADMASTER: And where is your tie, Darbishire?

DARBISHIRE: It's... oh, I'm sorry sir, I was using it as part of the special window-fastening device.

HEADMASTER: All of you are disgracefully untidy and dirty and I can't imagine why you choose to spend a half-holiday messing about in a puerile pursuit like this.

JENNINGS: No, sir.

HEADMASTER: What do you mean, "No, sir"? Are you disagreeing with what I said?

JENNINGS: No, sir, I meant no, you couldn't imagine why we – what you said, sir.

HEADMASTER: When I make a remark that is not a question, Jennings, neither answer nor comment is required. When I was your age I was content to spend my leisure time studying the poems of Tennyson and Wordsworth. Why can't you boys learn to do something like that?

JENNINGS: Er, - excuse me, sir, but do you want an answer to that, or is it just a no comment, sir?

HEADMASTER: I have come here to satisfy myself that the building of these huts does not infringe any of the school rules. Whose particular igloo is this sorry-looking affair composed of mud and bullrushes?

JENNINGS: Mine and Darbishire's, sir.

HEADMASTER: Mine and Darbisire's! I should have thought that the modicum of grammar which even you possess would have prompted you to say Darbishire's and mine.

JENNINGS: Yes, - er, I mean, no comment sir.

HEADMASTER: I'll inspect this one first. How does one enter?

JENNINGS: You'll have to kneel down, sir, and squeeze in through this hole; we're going to have a revolving door here when it's finished, but... oh sir, mind that puddle, sir, the front door's super marshy, sir.

HEADMASTER: The dampness in my knees has already informed me of that, Jennings.

DARBISHIRE: Excuse me, sir, I think you're kneeling on a newt, sir.

HEADMASTER: (*voice fading and muffled as he enters hut*) Kindly allow me to conduct investigations in my own way, Darbishire.

Pause

JENNINGS: (*whispering*) I say, this is ozard egg, isn't it? Who'd have thought he'd butt in like this?

TEMPLE: He's in a bit of a bait, too; I don't like the sound of him.

VENABLES: Surely he won't stop the huts. After all, Mr. Carter said it'd be all right if we didn't break any rules.

DARBISHIRE: We needn't despair yet, anyway. My father says that we should eschew excessive lamentation which avails.

JENNINGS: Yours would, Darbishire. Mine just says, "Why worry".

Dull thuds and scraping noises from hut

JENNINGS: Golly, what on earth's he doing in there?

HEADMASTER: (*muffled*) Come here, Jennings, quickly.

JENNINGS: Yes, sir.

More thuds and scrapings and a minor landslide

DARBISHIRE: Oh gosh, this is awful; what's happening?

Indistinguishable murmur of voices in hut between Jennings and the Headmaster

VENABLES: Have a dekko inside, Temple, and see what they're doing.

TEMPLE: It's all right, Jennings is coming back now... What's happened, Jen?

JENNINGS: Well, there's been a most unfortunate accident. Part of the wall's fallen in and the Head's got stuck in the back room boys' department and he can't move.

DARBISHIRE: Oh golly, what are we going to do?

VENABLES: He ought to have known he was too big to go in there.

JENNINGS: Of course he should. It was only built for small boffins.

TEMPLE: How are you going to get him out?

JENNINGS: He told me to send for Mr. Carter. Look, you go, Venables; I've just got to stop and help, 'cos if he goes on struggling like this, he'll smash the place up.

VENABLES: Okay, Jennings, I'll go.

JENNINGS: He's doing an awful lot of damage; he's put one foot through the prefabricated ventilating shaft already, and he's got the other one stuck in the emergency drinking water petrol tin.

DARBISHIRE: He's bound to stop the huts after this. My father says that one woe doth tread on another's heels so fast they...

JENNINGS: Here's Mr. Carter. Thank goodness he's come.

MR. CARTER: What's all this nonsense Venables has got hold of? Where's the Headmaster?

JENNINGS: He's inside, sir, and he's doing a smashing lot of dilapidations. It's beginning to look like our house at home after the Army had had it.

MR. CARTER: We'll have to take the roof off; that'll be quickest. Come on, you can all help.

Banging and cracking up of branches

It's all right, sir, we're nearly there; won't be a minute... There, you can get out now.

HEADMASTER: Ugh! Grmph! H'm. Thank you, Mr. Carter. Come here you boys. I have made my inspection, - a thorough inspection, I might add, at uncomfortably close quarters and what I found confirms my worst suspicions. In the front room, or vestibulum, I discovered a chisel, purloined from the carpenter's shop, which had obviously been used as a screwdriver. A school tooth mug was in use as a flower vase, a French text book blocked up a hole in the wall and two school dinner plates held a miscellaneous assortment of objects ranging from plasticine to secotine and earthworms to earwigs.

JENNINGS: We were going to take them all back, sir; the school things I mean like the plates and the chisel and we thought if we had the French book, sir, we could brush up our pronoun objects and things, sir.

HEADMASTER: You will hardly credit it, Mr. Carter, but worse was to come. Having inspected the vestibulum I proceeded to crawl, in a prone position, into the inner sanctum. Scarcely had I edged my head and shoulders through the aperture, when a portion of the edifice collapsed on the small of my back, pinning me to the ground in a welter of briars and brambles.

JENNINGS: I'm terribly sorry, sir; it's never done that with me and Darbishire, - er, I mean Darbishire and I, sir.

HEADMASTER: And finally, as my line of vision was limited to looking in one direction, insult was added to injury by my being confronted with a misspelt monstrosity, constructed of lemonade-bottle tops, bidding me welcome to the old-world hut in letters of red, orange and purple.

DARBISHIRE: That was my door mat, sir, and the spelling was all right really, 'cos it's medieval and my father says when you say "Ye" instead of "the", you're using the old Anglo-Saxon letter called thorn.

HEADMASTER: Upon a more suitable occasion, Darbishire, I shall be delighted to discuss medieval philology with you, but at the moment any mention of thorns, whether Anglo-Saxon or otherwise, merely serves to heighten the embarrassment of a very shattering experience.

DARBISHIRE: Yes, sir.

HEADMASTER: I have decided, therefore, to put this corner of the playing-fields out of bounds and in future no boys are to make huts.

MR. CARTER: It was my fault really, sir. I thought that properly supervised they'd be very good fun and might teach them something about...

HEADMASTER: Properly supervised, perhaps, but the master on duty can't be in six places at once and my chief objection is the appalling state these boys are getting into on this marshy ground. Look at them, Mr. Carter, muddy, dishevelled, untidy. These activities are undermining the pride they should be taking in their personal appearance and encouraging them to misuse school property in the most destructive way.

MR. CARTER: Yes, sir.

HEADMASTER: You boys will go and make yourselves tidy. After that you will spend an hour in tidying your desks, tidying the classrooms and tidying the school grounds.

OMNES: Yes, sir.

HEADMASTER: On my way over here, I noticed an accumulation of litter lying about on the quad; an apple core and two toffee papers to be precise. Tomorrow, I have a very important visitor coming to see the school and I intend to have the place tidy for his arrival. Go along now, and after tea I shall inspect the amount of litter that each of you has collected.

OMNES: Yes, sir.

HEADMASTER: I wonder if you'd mind having a good look round tonight Carter, and making sure that everything's spick and span. The servants will have to work overtime this evening and we'll have the whole building thoroughly ship-shape by tomorrow. Oh yes, and will you tell Matron that all the boys are to wear their best suits. It's a very special occasion. You see, I'm expecting Lord Falconbridge.

MR. CARTER: Really! You mean the Cabinet Minister?

HEADMASTER: Yes, he's got a young son, Talbot, whom he's bringing with him as he's looking for a prep school to send him to. Whether he decides to send the boy here next term will depend upon whether he is favourably impressed by his visit tomorrow. That's why I think a little extra effort is called for.

MR. CARTER: Yes, but don't you think it'd be better to let him see us as we are normally? All these best suits and spit and polish may give him a false impression.

HEADMASTER: In this case I think not. A Cabinet Minister expects a certain amount of ceremony and I think we should be failing in our duty if we didn't provide it. Besides, the occasion is very important. If I can persuade Lord Falconbridge to send Talbot here it'll be an excellent thing for the school. In less than no time we shall be recognised as being *the* school for the sons of the aristocracy.

MR. CARTER: I'm not sure that I'd like that. Sounds a trifle pompous.

HEADMASTER: But my dear Carter, think of the influential position we should hold. Yes, I'm determined to spare no effort in making a favourable impression on Lord Falconbridge tomorrow.

Fade to:

TEMPLE: How much rubbish have you collected, Darbishire?

DARBISHIRE: I can't find any more, Bod. I did have a smashing lot but I've been putting it in one of the waste paper baskets until I've got a whole heap; then I'll be able to take it to the Head.

TEMPLE: That's what I'm going to do, 'cos he'll expect us to show him quite a lot. If he's got over his bait about the huts he might even give a prize for the biggest collection. Gosh, look at that great pile Jennings has got! Where did you find all that, Jennings?

JENNINGS: I found it in the waste paper basket.

DARBISHIRE: But you can't have that. It's ours. We put it there.

JENNINGS: Well, the Head said find all you can and I found this.

TEMPLE: You pestilent oik, you've been pinching our litter.

JENNINGS: Fancy making a fuss about rubbish. What's it all about anyway?

TEMPLE: Carter says there's a Lord Somebody or other coming tomorrow. He's in the Cabinet.

JENNINGS: What, like the disappearing lady?

TEMPLE: No, the other sort and we've got to wear best suits and be spivish careful how we behave.

JENNINGS: How about if he talks to us. Do we have to call him Your Worship, or My Grace, or what?

DARBISHIRE: My father's got a book about that. Now, s'pose you want to write a letter to a high dignitary of the church; you have to start off "My Lord Bishop".

JENNINGS: But he isn't in the church, he's in the cabinet.

DARBISHIRE: I'm not sure how you talk to people in cabinets, but I know you finish off a letter to an ambassador by saying you're his excellency's most obedient servants.

JENNINGS: I should jolly well think we are. Look at all the orange peel and junk we've picked up for him.

DARBISHIRE: And my father's book's got a lot of other useful information, too. F'rinstance, did you know that the population of China was so big that if you put them in a long unbroken line and made them march, it'd take them twenty years, going day and night, for them all to go past you.

JENNINGS: How do they know? Has anyone ever done it?

DARBISHIRE: Well, I s'pose somebody must have done it once or they wouldn't know, would they?

JENNINGS: But that's goofy. What'd happen when their shoes wore out?

DARBISHIRE: They'd get new ones of course.

JENNINGS: But there wouldn't be anyone to make new ones 'cos they'd all be marching. They'd be super tired too if they had to march all that time without stopping.

DARBISHIRE: Don't be so wet. They'd have to sleep sometime.

JENNINGS: No they couldn't, 'cos you said without stopping and they'd hold the line up if they did and then there'd be a gap.

DARBISHIRE: Well p'raps there would be a gap then.

JENNINGS: Well, that proves that the book's wrong 'cos you said the line was unbroken.

TEMPLE: If you two don't stop nattering and do some more work, Lord What's-his-name'll have to wade ankle-deep in litter when he gets here tomorrow.

Fade out, pause and fade in, distant and approaching:

HEADMASTER: ...and I'm sure you will be most interested in these dormitories, Lord Falconbridge; we're particularly proud of them.

FALCONBRIDGE: (*bored*) Oh yes, yes, quite, of course. Most interesting.

HEADMASTER: Now these windows are all fitted with Vita glass which means that they allow all the vitamin B, - er, the infra red, the er, - that is...

TALBOT: You mean ultra violet rays.

FALCONBRIDGE: Be quiet, Talbot, when the Headmaster's speaking.

HEADMASTER: As I was saying, ultra violet. And every window you'll see is fitted with a Davey fire escape though fortunately, of course, we never have to use them.

TALBOT: How do you know they still work, then?

FALCONBRIDGE: Don't interrupt, Talbot. You were saying, Headmaster?

HEADMASTER: We're particularly proud of our overhead system of ventilation. Now, this ensures that there are no draughts and every boy obtains a minimum of three thousand, five hundred cubic yards of air. Or is it thirty thousand, five hundred cubic feet? Let me see, twenty-seven cubic feet equal a cubic yard and there are one thousand, seven hundred and twenty-eight cubic inches in a foot, so that makes...

FALCONBRIDGE: Yes, well please don't bother. I can see it's all perfectly splendid and most remarkable.

HEADMASTER: And in addition to that, Lord Falconbridge, you'll be interested to know that these dormitories are kept at an even temperature by heated panels let into the walls.

FALCONBRIDGE: Really! Most interesting, most interesting.

HEADMASTER: Now you've seen our oak-panelled dining hall facing south; did I tell you it was built on a sandy sub-soil?

FALCONBRIDGE: You did mention it, yes.

TALBOT: He told us three times, Daddy, when he was talking about the drains.

FALCONBRIDGE: That's enough, Talbot.

HEADMASTER: Now the next thing to see is our up-to-date kitchen. I'm sure you'll be interested in our thermostatically controlled washing up machine and our electrically-operated bread-slicer.

FALCONBRIDGE: I'm sure it'll be most interesting, most interesting.

HEADMASTER: And then I must show you the bathroom, tiled throughout, of course. Our up-to-date gymnasium and our heating device which ensures an even temperature for the water in the swimming bath; and our classrooms which...

TALBOT: I s'pose you have thermostic inkwells to keep the ink at boiling point and tincy-wincy dredgers to get the bits of blotting paper...

HEADMASTER: I-I-I really...

FALCONBRIDGE: Talbot! Really! I must apologise for my son, Headmaster. He's not been away from home before and he doesn't realise a Headmaster is a person who is entitled to er- um...

HEADMASTER: Quite, quite. Just Talbot's way of putting it, eh! Ha, ha, ha! But we'll soon be able to alter that next term, won't we? Oh yes, there won't be much difficulty about that.

TALBOT: But I don't want to come to this school.

FALCONBRIDGE: Now stop that, Talbot. That's for me to decide.

TALBOT: I don't like it, it's stuffy.

FALCONBRIDGE: I think he's getting a little bored of accompanying us. Perhaps if he could meet some boys of his own age, he'd feel happier about it.

HEADMASTER: Of course, of course. A personally conducted tour by some of his contemporaries. Now where did I see some boys? Ah yes (*receding and calling to distance*). Come here you two boys.

JENNINGS: (*approaching*) Yes, sir?

HEADMASTER: Oh, it's you and Darbishire! Well never mind, that can't be helped. This is Jennings, Lord Falconbridge.

FALCONBRIDGE: How d'you do, Jennings.

JENNINGS: How d'you do my... your... um, sir.

HEADMASTER: And this is Darbishire.

FALCONBRIDGE: How d'you do, Darbishire.

DARBISHIRE: Er, I beg to remain your Lordship's most obedient servant, sir.

HEADMASTER: Now, Jennings and Darbishire, I have a little job for you. This is Talbot Falconbridge, Lord Falconbridge's youngest son.

TALBOT: Hullo!

HEADMASTER: I want you to take him round the school and show him the things that will be of the greatest interest to him. Show him the library, the collection of sports trophies, the scholarship honours board and ah, perhaps the tuck shop, eh? Ha, ha, ha! Run along now... Well now, Lord Falconbridge, if you'll come this way I can show you our system of self-closing boot lockers.

FALCONBRIDGE: Oh really! Most interesting, most interesting!

Fade out. Pause. Fade in:

TALBOT: Well I don't call this library very exciting. Old encyclopaedias and things. Haven't you got anything worth reading?

DARBISHIRE: Well we have, but all the decent books are out and these Hentys are just kept here so the shelves won't look too bare. Nobody ever reads this lot though.

JENNINGS: What else had we got to show this chap, Darbi? We've shown him the silver cups, and the tuck shop's closed anyway.

DARBISHIRE: The Head said show him the scholarship honours board.

JENNINGS: Oh yes, well there it is, Talbot, on the wall look.

TALBOT: Oh! Am I s'posed to get excited about it?

JENNINGS: No, but the Head'll probably ask me whether I've shown it to you, so I'd better do it properly. H'm, 1923 G.H. Tomlinson, scholarship to Repton; 1924 R.K. Blenkinsop, scholarship to Marlborough, 1925 C.L.N. Hibbert-Jones, scholarship to Winchester; 1926...

TALBOT: (*yawns*) How much more is there?

JENNINGS: Only another twenty-two years.

TALBOT: I can't wait all that time.

JENNINGS: No, I mean on the board. We've only got to get up to 1948.

TALBOT: It's all pretty boring isn't it? Don't you ever do anything else at this school except read the encyclopaedias and scholarship boards?

DARBISHIRE: Well, we did have a smashing decent thing we used to do, but it got stopped yesterday.

TALBOT: What was that?

DARBISHIRE: We all built huts behind the pond; it was wizard.

JENNINGS: Our hut was the best, 'cos if you wanted to get to it the difficult way you had to use our bridge as far as it was built and jump the rest; and we had a control tower up a tree and you couldn't parachute off the bridge to the runway till you got a signal to come in and land.

DARBISHIRE: Yes, and our hut's got all sorts of modern labour saving devices, like string, so's you can pull it without having to get up. Honestly, Talbot, some of our things are supersonic.

TALBOT: Really? You mean they go faster than sound?

JENNINGS: Our pork pie will if we leave it much longer.

TALBOT: Do you have feeds in the huts, then?

JENNINGS: We were going to, but it's all off now. We thought of using the front door as a drawbridge and pulling it up and pretending we were besieged; then you see, if the siege had been going on for months we'd be so hungry that we wouldn't know if the pork pie tasted a bit off. And if we waited till next month we'd have our sweet rations and we could mix sherbet and stuff in with it, so's to disguise the taste.

TALBOT: Goody – goody – goody. Come on, let's go over to the hut.

JENNINGS: We can't; they're out of bounds now.

TALBOT: Well, if no one's allowed over there, no one'll see us. And, after all, the Head said you were to show me everything. Do let's go.

JENNINGS: It's terribly boggy in parts. You'd get delectably muddied up.

TALBOT: My father wouldn't mind that.

JENNINGS: P'raps not, but our Head would. What do you think, Darbishire?

DARBISHIRE: Well it should be quite safe, because the Head's busy with Lord Falconbridge and as Talbot's father's a lord that makes us his obedient servants really, so p'raps it's our duty if he wants to go.

JENNINGS: Okay, come on then. But we must try and keep clean.

Fade to:

JENNINGS: I think we'd better not go the difficult way over the bridge part, Talbot, 'cos of our best suits.

TALBOT: Oh but we must, Jennings. Is this the bridge? Oh isn't it super! Come on, I'm going first.

JENNINGS: Be careful then, 'cos it isn't all built yet and if the knots in the football bootlaces give way there'll be a most awful...

Sound of splash

Oh golly, he's fallen in. Are you all right, Talbot?

TALBOT: Yes thanks; I'll just get these tadpoles out of my collar.

JENNINGS: You shouldn't have pancaked till you got the signal from the control-tower.

TALBOT: Well, let's pretend I was a sea-plane then.

DARBISHIRE: You're terribly muddy. Whatever will your father say?

TALBOT: Well, so are you. It'll soon brush off.

JENNINGS: I vote that when we've shown him the huts, we nip off to the bathroom and clean up a bit, then everything'll be all right.

TALBOT: Where do we go from here? Through this hole in the hedge?... Ow. Help me through, Jennings.

JENNINGS: Come on, then. Oh golly, you've torn your trousers and your face is bleeding - well, it would be if it could get through the mud.

TALBOT: Never mind; I'm enjoying this.

DARBISHIRE: There'll be an awful row if we get copped.

JENNINGS: We shan't be, at least the Head won't be coming over here; at least I shouldn't think so – at least I hope he doesn't.

TALBOT: Is this the hut? Isn't it wizard!

JENNINGS: Well, it's all that's left of it after it collapsed on the Head. I don't know where half our gadgets have got to.

DARBISHIRE: We'd better make an inventory of what's left.

TALBOT: What's an inventory?

JENNINGS: It's a place where boffins invent things. There's not much left of our back room inventory now though.

TALBOT: I'm going to climb this tree.

JENNINGS: I shouldn't, it's not very safe... Well, be careful then, that branch you're on's going to...

Branch cracks. Tearing noise and thud as Talbot hits ground

Oh gosh. Are you all right, Talbot?

TALBOT: Yes, I'm fine, thanks. I haven't enjoyed myself so much for ages.

DARBISHIRE: Yes, but look at your coat. You've left part of it on the tree.

TALBOT: That doesn't matter. I've got another one at home.

DARBISHIRE: Yes, but what's the Head... I say Jen, after we've been to the bathroom, we'd better go to the sewing-room and see if they could patch things up a bit. You look dreadful, Talbot.

TALBOT: Well you're a nice one to criticise other people's appearances. You went into the boggy part up to your knees nearly and Jennings has got that green weedy-stuff all down his suit...

JENNINGS: Everything'll be all right if we can clear up first. I wonder how long the Head'll be taking your father round.

TALBOT: Hours I should think. He's as proud of his labour-saving devices as Darbishire is, only he makes long speeches about all of them. What's this petrol tin for? Is it part of your inventions, Darbishire?

DARBISHIRE: Yes, but we might as well empty it. There's no point in having a fire extinguisher when everything's wet through anyway.

JENNINGS: Look out, you oik. You're pouring it all over my feet.

DARBISHIRE: Sorry Jen. Oh look, I never knew it had tadpoles in it. Spivish good job we didn't have to use it as emergency drinking supply.

JENNINGS: Well now it can be the tribal tom-tom again. You see Talbot, we used to have little concerts in the hut; you know, drum solos and that sort of thing. Darbi and I can do a hairy famous duet with drum accompaniment.

TALBOT: Let's hear it then and I'll play the drum for you.

JENNINGS: You can try it if you like. Look, we sing "They're changing guards at Buckingham Palace", and you do four biffs on the drum.

TALBOT: Like this?

Four bangs on petrol can

JENNINGS: Yes. And you do that in between every line.

TALBOT: Okay.

JENNINGS: Come on, then Darbishire. One, two, three, go

JENNINGS: }   (*singing*) They're changing guards at

DARBISHIRE: }   Buckingham Palace.

Pause. Silence

JENNINGS: Go on, Talbot. Four beats.

TALBOT: Oh sorry, I thought there was a bit more.

JENNINGS: We'll start again. Ready, go.

JENNINGS: }   (*singing*) They're changing guards at

DARBISHIRE: }   Buckingham Palace.

Four beats on petrol can

JENNINGS: }   (*singing*) Christopher Robin went down with

DARBISHIRE: }   Alice.

Four beats

JENNINGS: }   (*singing*) Alice is marrying one of the guard…

DARBISHIRE: }

Four beats

JENNINGS: No, Talbot. We have to sing two lines there. Wait till we get to "hard".

TALBOT: You said between every line.

JENNINGS: Yes, but not that one. Come on, Darbi.

JENNINGS: }   (*singing*) Alice is marrying one of the guard,

DARBISHIRE: }   A soldier's life is terrible hard,

Four beats

JENNINGS: }   (*singing*) Says Alice.

DARBISHIRE: }

Pause. Silence

JENNINGS: Well go on; it's time for four biffs.

TALBOT: But you haven't sung enough yet. "Says Alice", isn't a line.

JENNINGS: Yes it is; it's a short one.

TALBOT: But that's goofy; you can't have a line with two words and then expect me to come in just after saying I didn't have to do four biffs till you'd sung two lines.

JENNINGS: We'll try the next verse. Now this time it's "we saw a guard in a sentry box; one of the sergeants looks after his socks". Ready, go.

JENNINGS: }   (*singing*) They're changing guards at

DARBISHIRE: }   Buckingham Palace…

TALBOT: You're wrong now. You said you were going to sing about a sentry box.

JENNINGS: That's later. Really, Talbot, you don't seem to have got any ear for music at all. Now let's get it right.

JENNINGS: }   (*singing*) They're changing guards at

DARBISHIRE: }   Buckingham Palace.

Four beats

Christopher Robin went down with Alice.

Four beats

We saw a guard in a sentry box

One of the sergeants looks after his socks.

Four beats and fade out. Pause and fade in:

HEADMASTER: ...so you see, Lord Falconbridge, by having very small classes we maintain a very high standard of academic work.

FALCONBRIDGE: Quite, quite. Most remarkable.

HEADMASTER: Our discipline, here, is based upon mutual respect and we do the best to encourage the boys to take a pride in their appearance. We're most particular about personal tidiness; neatly brushed hair, clean finger nails, well polished shoes. Take any boy at random, and you'll find him smartly turned out with a spick and span neatness that is without parallel in any school in the country.

FALCONBRIDGE: Yes, I'm sure I should. Most interesting, most interesting.

HEADMASTER: Well now, I think you've seen everything.

FALCONBRIDGE: Good, - I mean, thank you so much Headmaster, it's been very kind of you to take all this trouble. I enjoyed it immensely and I thought everything was very interesting and er, - most interesting.

HEADMASTER: And if you could let me know fairly soon whether Talbot is to come here next term, I should be more than grateful.

FALCONBRIDGE: I can tell you now, Headmaster.

HEADMASTER: Splendid, splendid. May I enter him for next term, then?

FALCONBRIDGE: No, I'm afraid not.

HEADMASTER: Oh, that's most disappointing. I thought after you'd seen our up-to-date premises, that you'd be sure to be impressed by it all.

FALCONBRIDGE: Oh, I was. And the impression I got was that you had invented a machine for turning out tidy little boys with well-groomed hair and smartly knotted bootlaces.

HEADMASTER: Yes, but really, Lord Falconbridge...

FALCONBRIDGE: Now please don't be offended. You see I went through all this business of being polished till I shone when I was a boy, and frankly I hated it. And I decided that any son of mine should have a chance to develop in happy surroundings where he could behave naturally if he felt like it. In short, Headmaster, impressive though your vita-glass windows and your heated wall-panels may be, I feel that Talbot would be happier making mud-pies out of your sandy sub-soil, than merely standing on it without getting his shoes dirty.

HEADMASTER: Oh! Well in that case, there's nothing more to be said. Now we'd better find Talbot. Let me see, they're probably admiring the portraits of the former Headmasters in the West wing. Ah, here's Mr. Carter, perhaps he knows. Carter, have you seen Jennings and Darbishire?

MR. CARTER: Yes, sir, they went over towards the huts a little while ago.

HEADMASTER: But that's out of bounds. Didn't you stop them?

MR. CARTER: They had Lord Falconbridge's son with them, so I assumed they were taking him with your permission.

HEADMASTER: Certainly not; I gave no permission for that. I think we'd better go over there, Lord Falconbridge.

Fade to singing, distant. Bring up slowly:

JENNINGS: }   (*singing*) They're changing the guards at
DARBISHIRE: }   Buckingham Palace.

Four beats on petrol can

Christopher Robin went down with Alice.

Four beats

A face looked out, but it wasn't the King's,
He's much too busy a-signing things,

Four beats

Says Alice.

Bring up singing to normal volume. Four beats

They're changing guards at Buckingham Palace.

Four beats

Christopher Robin went down with Alice.

Four beats

Do you think the king knows all about...

Break off suddenly

JENNINGS: Oh, gosh!
DARBISHIRE: Oh, gosh!
TALBOT: Hullo, Daddy, we're having a super delectable prang.

TALBOT: Hullo, Daddy, we're having a super delectable prang.
HEADMASTER: Well... I... good gracious... bless my... words fail me!

HEADMASTER: Well... I... good gracious... bless my... words fail me!

JENNINGS: (*whisper*) We've had it, Darbi; there's going to be the most supersonic hoo-hah.

HEADMASTER: Jennings and Darbishire, come here. I have never in the course of my professional career, seen three boys in a more appallingly revolting state. What do you mean by allowing Lord Falconbridge's son to get into that condition? His jacket's torn, his tie's missing, his trousers are split, his shirt's wringing wet, his leg is bleeding and his shoes are smothered in ooze. And you two are nearly as bad. What do you mean by it?

JENNINGS: Nothing, sir; we were just trying to be his lordship's most obedient servants.

TALBOT: Daddy, this school is a wonderful place. There couldn't be anything better in the whole world than playing at huts, and Darbishire's a boffin and makes...

FALCONBRIDGE: You certainly seem to have been enjoying yourself, Talbot.

TALBOT: Yes I have, Daddy. Daddy, I can come to this school next term, can't I?

HEADMASTER: H'm. Jennings and Darbishire, you will take Talbot to Matron immediately. Tell her that he's to have a bath and his clothes are to be mended and dried at once. The same applies to you two, and when you are presentable, you will report to my study. I intend to deal with this breech of discipline with the utmost severity.

JENNINGS: Yes sir; I'm very sorry Lord, - your worship.

DARBISHIRE: So am I, my grace; we hoped to clean up before we saw you, you see.

FALCONBRIDGE: That's quite all right.

HEADMASTER: Run along now, all three of you and find Matron.

JENNINGS: Yes, sir.

Pause

HEADMASTER: I'm most terribly sorry this has happened, Lord Falconbridge; I assure you, I shall deal with Jennings and Darbishire very drastically indeed. An occurrence of this sort is very rare here, I assure you.

FALCONBRIDGE: Don't apologise, Headmaster. The fact that it can happen here is enough for me. I've changed my mind. If you'll accept him, I shall be very pleased to send Talbot to this school next term.

HEADMASTER: What? But I thought you said...?

FALCONBRIDGE: Yes I did, but I was judging you by the parade ground reception you gave me. All those boys in their best suits gave me the horrors, but the sight of those three thoroughly enjoying themselves rather restored the balance.

HEADMASTER: Well we did make a rather special effort for your visit. I must admit that normally we tend to become less formal than our tour of the school seemed to indicate. All the same, Jennings' behaviour...

FALCONBRIDGE: You'll have to forgive him Headmaster. In fact, I think he deserves a reward, because I should never have decided to send Talbot here if they hadn't shown me the more human side of school life. And, now he's made friends, Talbot is very keen to come.

Fade out. Pause. Fade in:

JENNINGS: (*subdued*) Go on, Darbishire; bags you knock on the study door.

DARBISHIRE: No; bags you. I haven't got the courage.

JENNINGS: One of us has got to.

DARBISHIRE: Well, you then. D'you think we'll get a swishing?

JENNINGS: Bound to, after a thing like that. Of course, it would be summer, wouldn't it?

DARBISHIRE: What's that got to do with it?

JENNINGS: We're only wearing thin underpants and it hurts more. D'you think Matron would let us put our winter-weights on, just for now?

DARBISHIRE: Come on, let's get it over.

Door knock

HEADMASTER: (*within*) Come in.

Door opens

Yes?

JENNINGS: Please, sir, you told us to come and see you, sir.

HEADMASTER: Ah yes, of course.

JENNINGS: Please, sir, we're very sorry we made such a mess of Talbot, sir.

HEADMASTER: Well, it had its compensations; and you'll be pleased to hear that he'll be joining you here next term.

JENNINGS: Yes, sir.

HEADMASTER: I've been thinking over this question of huts and I have decided that, properly supervised, they would provide excellent opportunities for you to develop a knowledge of woodcraft and bird-watching, and perhaps an occasional picnic might not come amiss, eh?

JENNINGS: Yes, sir, of course sir, but I thought, sir...

HEADMASTER: So to start the ball rolling, I suggest you go over this evening and repair the ravages occasioned by my visit. Oh yes, and my wife has managed to find this fresh pork pie and I thought you might like to take it, in case you felt the need for a little something.

JENNINGS: Thank you, sir.

DARBISHIRE: Thank you very much, sir.

HEADMASTER: Not at all; your assistance this afternoon, as guides, was so successful that I feel it deserves some recognition. Run along now, both of you.

Door opens and shuts. Pause

JENNINGS: You know, Darbishire, I think all grown-ups are as crazy as coots. One minute they're in a supersonic bait and there's a hefty hoo-hah going on and you're going to get a swishing and the next minute they're saying thank you ever so and handing out pork pies.

DARBISHIRE: I think you're right, Jen. At a certain age they all become sea-lion.

JENNINGS: All what?

DARBISHIRE: Something like that; er, - no, not sea-lion, senile.

JENNINGS: I should think the Head's definitely senile by now; he must be at least thirty; more than that, p'raps, even; seventy-five or eighty. Never mind, let's go and eat this pork pie.

Fade out.

JENNINGS
AND THE UNWELCOME GIFT

(First series no.6)

Jennings and the Unwelcome Gift was the sixth Jennings play.

It was first broadcast by the BBC Home Service for Children's Hour on 5th February 1949, with the following cast:

JENNINGS	John Charlesworth
DARBISHIRE	Loris Somerville
MR. CARTER	Geoffrey Wincott
MR. WILKINS	Wilfred Babbage
FRENCH FISHERMAN	Guy de Monceau

Fade in bell ringing, distant

MR. CARTER: Right, stop working and put your books away, quietly.

Shuffling of papers and books. A desk lid slams

I said, quietly, Jennings.

JENNINGS: I'm sorry, sir, it slipped.

MR. CARTER: Sit up and listen to me. Today, the Headmaster's decided to grant the half-holiday that he promised in honour of Ackroyd Major winning a scholarship.

Clapping

DARBISHIRE: Good old Ackroyd! I'll put you on my cake list, Ackroyd, honestly I will.

JENNINGS: Sir, will the school get a half-holiday if I ever win a scholarship?

MR. CARTER: The contingency is so remote, Jennings, that it hardly enters the sphere of practical politics.

JENNINGS: What's that mean, sir?

MR. CARTER: It means that you've got as much chance of winning a scholarship as that inkwell.

JENNINGS: Oh, sir.

DARBISHIRE: And if he did win one, sir, we'd all need six weeks half-holiday to get over the shock.

MR. CARTER: For today's half, there'll be cricket for those who want to play and a photographic competition for the boys who belong to the camera club.

JENNINGS: Oh, wizzo!

MR. CARTER: You will be allowed out, in twos, to take photos in the woods or the village, or down by the harbour. The subject of your photo can either be still life, or...

JENNINGS: What's that mean, sir?

MR. CARTER: A plant or a tree; anything that's alive, but doesn't move.

DARBISHIRE: Like Jennings doing his prep, sir?

MR. CARTER: Be quiet, Darbishire; or you can take something like yachts in the harbour, or a farmyard scene. You must develop your own photos in the darkroom and there'll be a

132

prize for the best entry. So during lunch, I want you to decide where you're going this afternoon, as you'll have to report to me before you leave.

Fade out. Pause. Fade in ship's siren

DARBISHIRE: It was a prang idea coming to the harbour, Jennings. Temple and Atkinson and all of them have gone into the woods.

JENNINGS: They'll only get photos of toadstools and things; we might get an aircraft carrier or a cruiser.

DARBISHIRE: What, in this harbour? Don't be so goofy, it's only got a titchy little wooden jetty. Anything bigger than a yacht would get stuck.

JENNINGS: Well, p'raps they will get stuck. It'd make a smashing photo, wouldn't it, two battleships jammed in the mouth of the harbour?

DARBISHIRE: Well, there aren't any battleships, so what shall we take?

JENNINGS: Look, there's a French fishing boat over there, with a man mending nets. Let's take him.

DARBISHIRE: How d'you know it's French?

JENNINGS: It's got "Boulogne" on the back.

DARBISHIRE: You are ignorant, Jennings; you don't have backs on ships; you mean abaft.

JENNINGS: It's French, anyway.

DARBSIHIRE: Abaft isn't French; it's English for the wide end.

JENNINGS: No, I mean it's a French fishing-boat. They do come in sometimes to shelter from the weather. He'd make a wonderful picture, wouldn't he? He's so dirty and he hasn't shaved for ages; much more super than photos of toadstools and things. I vote we ask him if we can go on board and take a snap.

DARBISHIRE: Go on, then; you ask him; I don't like to.

JENNINGS: *(calling)* Er, - excuse me, but would you mind frightfully if we came on board and took a photo of you?

FRENCH FISHERMAN: *(distant) Comment?*

DARBISHIRE: What did he say?

JENNINGS: I think he said "come on".

DARBISHIRE: No, he said "*comment*"; that means how much, or how many, or something, in French.

JENNINGS: I only want to take one.

DARBISHIRE: Tell him, then.

JENNINGS: (*calling*) Only one!

FISHERMAN: (*distant*) *Comment?*

JENNINGS: It can't mean how many, 'cos I've just told him that and he's said it again. P'raps he does mean "come on". Let's go, anyway; we can go down this ladder, look, and get on to the abaft part... Mind my fingers, Darbi; you keep treading on them.

DARBISHIRE: This ladder's wizard slippery; don't drop the camera... Now we're all right. Go on, Jen, ask him again.

JENNINGS: Good afternoon; we wondered if you'd mind posing for a photograph, because we're going in for a competition.

FISHERMAN: *Comment?*

JENNINGS: We can't come on any more; we're abaft already.

FISHERMAN: *Pardon?*

DARBISHIRE: He's deaf, Jen. Either that or he doesn't speak English. Try it louder.

JENNINGS: That's no good, if he doesn't understand.

DARBISHIRE: Anyone can understand English if you shout loud enough.

JENNINGS: All right. (*Loudly*) Please can I take your photo?

FISHERMAN: *Je ne comprends pas; suis Francais; je ne parle pas Anglais du tout.*

DARBISHIRE: You couldn't have been loud enough, Jennings.

FISHERMAN: *Moi, pas comprendre; suis Francais; moi, pas parler Anglais.*

JENNINGS: It's no good, Darbi; we'll have to talk to him in French.

DARBISHIRE: Go on, then.

JENNINGS: You do it; you were fifth in French last term and I was only one from bottom. Go on, say, "Can we take your photo"?

DARBISHIRE: "Can we", that's *pouvoir*, isn't it? *Je peux, tu peux, il peut, nous pouvons*, - that's it. Er -, h'm; *pouvons-nous prendre votre...* I don't know what photograph is.

FRENCH FISHERMAN: Comment?
DARBISHIRE: What did he say?
JENNINGS: I think he said "come on".

FISHERMAN: *Qu'est-ce qu'il raconte?*

DARBISHIRE: I think he's asking you what I said, Jennings. P'raps he doesn't understand my accent if he hasn't had a very good education. You try; say we're going to go in for a competition and...

JENNINGS: I can't; that'd mean using *aller* and if he hasn't had a good education he might not understand irregular verbs.

FISHERMAN: *Vous voulez quelque chose, hien?*

JENNINGS: Er, - *oui*, er, - *non*. Look here, Darbi, can't you say we want a fisherman's photo?

DARBISHIRE: I'll have a shot. Er, - *Monsieur.* Wait a sec, it's *vouloir*, isn't it? Er, - *nous voulons du poisson...*

FISHERMAN: *Ben oui; vous voulez du poisson? Attendez.*

JENNINGS: Where's he beetling off to?

DARBISHIRE: I'm afraid I put it rather badly. I meant to say "*pecheur*", 'cos that means fisherman, but in the heat of the moment, I said "*poisson*".

JENNINGS: You mean you called him a fish and he's got insulted and gone off?

DARBISHIRE: No, but I think he thinks we want some fish.

JENNINGS: You are a coot, Darbi. Fifth in French last term and you can't even talk to a man who probably hasn't even looked at a French grammar book since he left school.

DARBISHIRE: Well, I bet I know the list of irregular comparison of adjectives and indirect pronoun objects as well as he does.

JENNINGS: Fat lot of good that is if you can't explain the difference between a fisherman and a fish. Never mind, I've got a photo of him.

DARBISHIRE: You've got it? Oh, rare! When?

JENNINGS: When you were telling him he was a fish.

DARBISHIRE: I didn't say that; I said... oh, never mind; how did you get it?

JENNINGS: Well I knew that if I waited until you'd gone through all your past participles, I should never get it; so I just took it when he wasn't looking. Should be rather coy, if it comes out. He was smiling in a puzzled sort of way, and messing about with a hole in the net.

DARBISHIRE: Oh, smashing! I'm glad it's over. The strain of talking in a foreign tongue was beginning to tell on me. Can we go now? He doesn't seem to be coming back.

JENNINGS: All right, then... Oh, gosh, look, he is coming back. Heavens! He's got both hands full of fish; must be a dozen, at least.

FISHERMAN: *Voila, mon vieux. Du poisson pour votre maman.*

JENNINGS: Oh, er, - they're not for me, are they?... I hope.

FISHERMAN: *Ben si; rapportez-les pour la soupe.*

DARBISHIRE: Well, go on, Jennings, he wants you to take them; he's holding them out to you.

JENNINGS: Oh, er, - thanks frightfully; *merci beaucoup.*

FISHERMAN: *Ces pour votre maman. Vous comprenez?* You geef ze feesh at your mozzer.

JENNINGS: I don't think we've got a mozzer to give it at; er, - to.

FISHERMAN: *Comment?*

DARBISHIRE: What he means, Jen, is that we're to take the fish home to our mothers.

JENNINGS: Tell him you don't have mothers at boarding school and we don't know who else to give it to.

DARBISHIRE: I couldn't possibly; there's too many negative interrogatives and partitive articles and things in what you said. My father says that to know one's limitations is the first...

FISHERMAN: *Pardon?*

JENNINGS: He wants you to translate what you just said, Darbishire.

DARBISHIRE: Oh golly; h'm. *Mon pere dit que...* oh, it's no good, Jen. Take the fish and let's go.

JENNINGS: But I don't want the wretched things. What can I do with them?

DARBISHIRE: That doesn't matter. They're a gift; he thinks we've asked for them and he'll be spivish offended if we don't take them with us.

JENNINGS: Okay. Er, - *merci pour les poissons, Monsieur. Bonjour.*

DARBISHIRE: *Bonjour, Monsieur. Je crois que vos poissons sont charmants.*

138

FISHERMAN: *Au 'voir; au 'voir.*

Fade to:

JENNINGS: Go on, Darbi; it's your turn to carry them now.

DARBISHIRE: No fear; I did all the talking. If you're such a nitwit that you can't hold an intelligent conversation in French, the least you can do is carry the beastly fish without moaning.

JENNINGS: They're so smash-on slippery. I keep dropping them and I can't get any more in my pockets. Anyway, if your French hadn't been so oikish, you could have explained that we didn't want them. Dash it all, Darbi, what are we going to do? It was all very well not wanting to offend him, but we can't take this lot back to school with us.

DARBISHIRE: Why not? There's no rule about it is there?

JENNINGS: I expect so; there's rules about everything like that. Rule number nine million and forty-seven; any boy walking into school carrying nine large, raw, slippery fishes weighing six hundredweight, shall be liable to receive a super delectable swishing. By order.

DARBISHIRE: How'd it be if we foxed them into our tuck-boxes and then, when we go home at the end of term we could give them to our mothers like the man said.

JENNINGS: You may think yourself a smashing French interpretator, Darbi, but you've got about as much sense as this fish that keeps giving me a look; can't you imagine what they'd be like by the end of term?

DARBISHIRE: I vote we throw them away, then.

JENNINGS: Someone might see; then we'd be had up for wasting food or cruelty to dumb chums or something... I know what! We'll smuggle them back to school and eat them before brekker tomorrow.

DARBISHIRE: What... raw!

JENNINGS: No, you coot; don't be so bogus. Look, we've got to develop our film for the photo competition, so that means we can use the dark room. Well, there's a gas ring in there, 'cos I've tried it and we'll fry the fish and no one can come in while we're doing it, 'cos that'd spoil the film.

DARBISHIRE: Coo, yes, super-duper! There's a rule you're not allowed to open the door, 'cos of letting the light in... Yes, but what are we going to fry them in?

JENNINGS: What about using one of those developing dishes, if we poured the hypo out first? And we've got to have some lard, or something, haven't we?

DARBISHIRE: I've got a tin of vaseline that Matron gave me to put on my sore heel.

JENNINGS: That'd do, wizardly.

DARBISHIRE: Yes, it is rather a good idea, isn't it? Good idea; *bon idee*. There you are, my French is tons better already just from having a little informal chat with a native.

JENNINGS: Don't be so goofy, Darbishire. He wasn't a native, he was a Frenchman.

DARBISHIRE: He must have been both, mustn't he, if he was a native of France?

JENNINGS: He couldn't have been, 'cos natives don't speak French. They say "wallah-wallah" and "m'bongo-m'bongo".

DARBISHIRE: Those aren't natives; they're negroes. And this chap was a Frenchman.

JENNINGS: Well, according to you, then, all Frenchmen are negroes.

DARBISHIRE: Natives of France aren't, unless they come from French Equatorial Africa, so that proves... Golly, look out; there's Mr. Carter.

JENNINGS: Gosh, yes, we've got back quicker than I thought. Look, you take these other fish and put them in your pocket; then we can both walk past him with nothing showing.

DARBISHIRE: All right... Oh, golly, they'll make my pockets super mucky won't they?

JENNINGS: It can't be helped. After all, I've got liquorice allsorts and no end of stuff mixed up with mine. Lord knows what it'll taste like.

DARBISHIRE: I've got them all in except this one. What shall I do with it?

JENNINGS: Put it under your cap.

DARBISHIRE: Under my...? Oh no.

JENNINGS: Why not; you can wash your hair when you go to bed.

DARBISHIRE: Oh, I wasn't worrying about that; I just thought, s'posing it slips out.

JENNINGS: Pull your cap down firmly and don't mess about with it... Hurry up, he'll see us in a minute... That's all right. Of course, it'd be better still if Mr. Carter'd got a cold.

DARBISHIRE: Why?

JENNINGS: Well, I don't know about me, Darbishire, but I could tell there's something fishy about you from half a mile off.

JENNINGS: } Good afternoon, sir.

DARBISHIRE: }

MR. CARTER: Good afternoon. H'm. Jennings, I see, has been properly brought up, but the same can't be said for Darbishire. Can't you raise your cap, Darbishire? Is it glued to your head?

DARBISHIRE: It's ...it's not exactly glued, no, sir.

MR. CARTER: Then why doesn't it come off when you meet a master?

DARBISHIRE: Well, I did sort of tweak the peak, sir.

JENNINGS: I think Darbishire meant it as a naval salute, sir. You see, we've been down to the harbour and you get out of the way of raising it when you've been amongst yachting caps and sou'westers and things.

MR. CARTER: You don't have to tell me where you've been; you're standing to windward of me and it's only too obvious. However, as it's a half-holiday, I'll be tactful and change the subject. Have you taken a photo for the competition?

JENNINGS: Yes sir, we've got a smashing snap of a native. Well, Darbishire says he was, but he was white, really; or he would have been if he'd had a wash.

DARBISHIRE: Yes sir, it was supersonic. He was an alien, but I found I knew his lingo fairly well, so I was able to have quite a little pow-wow with him.

JENNINGS: Darbishire's just swanking, sir. He was a Frenchman and Darbishire told him he was a fish.

MR. CARTER: That must have been very comforting for him. There's nothing like a friendly word to make a foreigner feel at home in a strange land.

JENNINGS: That's what we thought, sir, so we were specially careful not to do anything to offend him.

MR. CARTER: Quite; I've no doubt he was highly delighted at being called a fish.

DARBISHIRE: Sir, I didn't, sir. Jennings' French was so hopeless, sir, he couldn't follow what I was talking about.

MR. CARTER: Unless he was a thought-reader, I don't suppose the Frenchman could, either.

DARBISHIRE: His French wasn't very good, sir. At least he said a lot of things very fast that weren't in the French grammar book, but he hadn't got much idea of partitive articles and disjunctive pronouns at all, sir. As for the subjunctive, it might have been a closed book to him.

JENNINGS: P'raps he hasn't got up to it yet. All the same, I wouldn't mind getting him to help me with my French prep.

MR. CARTER: Well, it's nearly tea time, so I suggest you try and remove some of the salty tang of the ocean that seems to be pervading the atmosphere.

JENNINGS: Yes, sir.

MR. CARTER: Oh, and by the way, I said that as this was a half-holiday I wouldn't ask awkward questions, but you might remember that although fish is good for the brain, I doubt whether the entire catch of the French herring industry would enable you to win a scholarship overnight; so don't try it.

JENNINGS: I don't understand what you mean, sir.

MR. CARTER: No? Well, here's a tip for your before I go on duty and start being official. Dug well into the ground, fish makes an excellent fertiliser for the soil, but kept above ground for too long, it's likely to invite investigation by the sanitary inspector.

Fade out. Pause. Fade in door opening and shutting

JENNINGS: That's right, Darbi; now bolt it.

Door bolted

Good; now we're all right. It's only half-past six, so we'll have masses of time to do the cooking and eating before anyone's up.

DARBISHIRE: But we'll be expected to have developed the photo.

JENNINGS: I did that last night; it's come out wizardly. I'll be able to give it in to Mr. Carter when it's dry.

DARBISHIRE: I say, you don't think he suspected anything yesterday afternoon, do you? All that talk about fish being a brain

142

fertiliser or something, d'you think he was giving us a chance to get rid of it?

JENNINGS: What, and waste good food? We'd be crackers to bury it. Besides, how could he have known anything? We'd got it stowed where he couldn't possibly have seen it.

DARBISHIRE: Well, that one under my cap; there was a fin or something tickling my ear and I wondered whether...

JENNINGS: Oh, rubbish! Come on, let's get on with this job. We'll use this developing dish and I've got the fish in this bag, look; and I borrowed some matches from the kitchen. Have you got the vaseline?

DARBISHIRE: Yes, but there wasn't much left, so I brought some cold cream and my cricket-bat oil as well.

JENNINGS: You're sure bat oil isn't poisonous?

DARBISHIRE: 'Course it isn't. All the best spivish hotels and places use it for frying.

JENNINGS: Okay, then. I'll just clean this dish out before we start; we don't want it tasting of hypo.

DARBISHIRE: Gosh, no; we must keep it pure. It was a massive brainwave of yours, Jennings, this cookery stunt, 'cos although it was super decent of the fisherman to give it to us, if we couldn't have eaten it, it'd just be a white elephant.

JENNINGS: What'd be a white elephant?

DARBISHIRE: This fish that we're going to cook, would.

JENNINGS: Listen, Darbishire, it's quite enough trouble cooking fish without starting in on white elephants as well.

DARBISHIRE: Still, you must admit it was decent of him... I wonder why they always look as though they need a bath.

JENNINGS: Well, the dirt shows up more than it does on ordinary ones. Besides, look at all the area they've got to keep clean.

DARBISHIRE: I s'pose they wouldn't look so bad if they didn't wear those filthy blue overalls with patches on them.

JENNINGS: Don't be completely bogus, Darbishire; white elephants don't wear blue overalls.

DARBISHIRE: I never said they did; I was talking about French fishermen. Anyone with any sense knows there's no such thing as a white elephant, really.

JENNINGS: You said there was; you said our fish was one.

143

DARBISHIRE: I meant it metaphysically; white elephants are just figures of speech, like similes and hypobowls.

JENNINGS: The proper word for this thing I'm trying to get clean is a developing dish; only an ignorant coot would call them hypo bowls.

DARBISHIRE: Not that sort of hypobowl. I mean figures of speech.

JENNINGS: Well, a minute ago, you meant white elephants. First the fish was one, then the developing dish. Some people don't know what they're talking about... Ah, that's clean; I hope; put the blackout curtain over the window and we'll get going.

DARBISHIRE: But we shan't be able to see.

JENNINGS: Yes, we shall, when I light the gas ring. After all, s'pose anyone was outside, they'd know we weren't developing a film if we hadn't got the blackout up.

DARBISHIRE: All right.

Curtains drawn. Match and gas ring lighted

JENNINGS: There we are. Now, we'll put the oil and the vaseline in the developing dish and get it all hot before we pop the fish in.

DARBISHIRE: Isn't this the prangest of prangs? What are you doing now? It's hairy murky in here with the blackout up, rather like what my father would call the cloistered seclusion of a cathedral's precincts, only...

Whoosh of minor explosion

JENNINGS: Oooh!... Ow!... Oh, gosh!

DARBISHIRE: Help! What's happening?... Look out, Jen, you'll set the place on fire.

JENNINGS: (*breathless*) It's all right, now; at least, I hope so. It's burnt itself out with a swoosh.

DARBISHIRE: What happened?

JENNINGS: Well, that developing dish was made of celluloid and when I put it on the gas ring, it just went swoosh.

DARBISHIRE: You are a dangerous maniac, Jennings; everyone knows celluloid's inflammable.

JENNINGS: Well, how could I see it was celluloid in the dark?

Both cough, continue intermittently

Gosh, these fumes are awful; the whole room's full of smoke. Open the window, quick, Darbi, or we'll asphyxiate.

DARBISHIRE: I don't think you can say we'll asphyxiate, 'cos it's a transitive verb; you can only *be* asphyxiated.

JENNINGS: That's what I'm being. Open the window, quick; it's pitch dark now the gas is out, and even if it wasn't, we couldn't see with all this smoke.

DARBISHIRE: Okay.

Window opened

Whew! That's better! Doesn't fresh air smell nice and clean? It's a wizard day outside, too. (*Sings*) Oh, what a beautiful morning; Oh what a beau... oh, golly!

Window slammed shut

JENNINGS: What's the matter? What have you shut the window for? We haven't cleared the air yet.

DARBISHIRE: Mr. Wilkins is outside. He saw my head pop out.

JENNINGS: Oh, corks! And he must have wondered why it popped in again so quick, too.

Tapping on window

Golly, he's tapping. He wants us to open the window. Pretend we haven't heard. He can't see in, anyway, 'cos of the blackout.

DARBISHIRE: He'll come round to the door, then. And he knows we can't be developing, 'cos of me opening the window.

More tapping on window

JENNINGS: We can't keep him out very long. We'll have to hide the fish, that's all, so he doesn't see it. Where can I put the bag?

DARBISHIRE: There's nowhere here you can. And what about the smoke and stuff?

JENNINGS: Shh! I think I heard him go away. He's probably going round to the door. Open the window, now, quick, and let the fumes out.

Window opened

We ought to fan it with something. Try flapping your coat about.

DARBISHIRE: I don't like this. My father says that...

Knocking on door

MR. WILKINS: (*without*) Open this door, at once!

145

JENNINGS: Oh, golly, where shall I put the bag of fish?

DARBISHIRE: Can't you slip it underneath your jacket and then sort of edge it round to the back?

JENNINGS: I'll have to; it's the only thing to do, but it's spivish tricky... All right, now open the door.

More knocking on door

MR. WILKINS: I told you to open this door...

Bolt withdrawn; door opens and Mr. Wilkins at normal volume

...immediately. Now, what's going on in here? Phew! Has there been something burning?

JENNINGS: Yes, sir, a developing dish caught fire, by accident; but it's all right now, sir.

MR. WILKINS: Is it! I'm not so sure. I don't know much about photography, and if it's necessary to befoul the air for miles around, I don't want to. Does Mr. Carter know you're in here?

JENNINGS: Well, I don't actually think he knows we're in here, at the moment, sir, if you see what I mean.

MR. WILKINS: So you're here without permission?

JENNINGS: In a matter of speaking, I s'pose we are, sir.

MR. WILKINS: Never mind the manner of speaking, or I'll do some speaking in a manner you won't appreciate. Furthermore, you're not allowed to get up before the rising-bell. That's two rules you've broken, in addition to nearly setting the place on fire. Go up to my room and wait there till I come. I want to make sure no damage has been done in this darkroom.

Fade out. Pause. Fade in:

DARBISHIRE: Did he say, "go in", Jennings, or wait outside the door?

JENNINGS: We'd better go in; he'll be up here in a minute and I've got to find somewhere to put this wretched fish.

DARBISHIRE: Bung it out of the window.

JENNINGS: Oh yes! Straight into the Head's garden; no, thank you.

DARBISHIRE: Well, you must hide it somewhere. Isn't there anywhere you could put it, just for now, and come back and get it later on?

JENNINGS: Let's go in and have a look.

Door opens

There's nowhere in here, is there? Those bookshelves are screwed to the wall, look, and I expect his desk's locked.

DARBISHIRE: Yes, it is; so's this cupboard. Pity they don't give masters more furniture, isn't it? Why couldn't you have got rid of it on the way up here?

JENNINGS: There was nowhere to put it. I did think of slipping it inside the grandfather clock in the hall, only Matron beetled into view just as I was going to.

DARBISHIRE: Well, it'll have to stay inside your jacket.

JENNINGS: It can't, possibly. He'd see it bulge. It was all right in the darkroom, but up here...

DARBISHIRE: Oh goodness, I think I can hear him coming.

JENNINGS: Go and have a squint, Darbi, quick.

DARBISHIRE: Yes, but what are you going to do with...

JENNINGS: Oh, go on, Darbi.

DARBISHIRE: All right, but, oh golly, isn't this awful! There'll be the most supersonic hoo-hah if he finds out.

Pause. Fade in footsteps distant

MR. WILKINS: *(distant)* Where's Jennings, Darbishire?

DARBISHIRE: *(distant)* He's waiting inside your room, sir.

MR. WILKINS: *(approaching)* I didn't tell you to wait in my room, Jennings. I meant outside.

JENNINGS: Sorry, sir.

MR. WILKINS: Fortunately, there doesn't seem to be much... What's the matter, Darbishire; have you lost something?

DARBISHIRE: Er, - no, sir.

MR. WILKINS: Then stop peering around the room in that idiotic fashion and listen to me, I was saying that, fortunately for you, there doesn't seem to be anything wrong with the darkroom, except a somewhat pungent aroma of photographic chemicals. Why anyone wants to indulge in a hobby that produces fumes, is beyond me, but there it is. There is, however, the fact that you were there without permission and before the rising-bell. Have you got your conduct books on you?

DARBISHIRE: Yes, sir, here's mine.

JENNINGS: I've got mine on me somewhere, sir; I shall have to turn my pockets out.

MR. WILKINS: Hurry up, then. Darbishire, what's the matter with you? Are the contents of Jennings' pockets such a novel sight that you have to gape like a village idiot?

DARBISHIRE: Er, no, sir.

JENNINGS: Here it is, sir.

MR. WILKINS: Right. Leave them with me. You'll both get the maximum stripes for each offence. Now go back to your dormitory and wait till it's time to get up.

Door opens and shuts. Pause

JENNINGS: Well, that wasn't so bad, was it?

DARBISHIRE: But... but where on earth was the fish?

JENNINGS: Oh, that! Well, I had a rather rare brainwave when you went out to see if Wilkie was coming; or rather, it wasn't so much a brainwave as that I hefty well had to do something, quick.

DARBISHIRE: And what did you do, quick?

JENNINGS: I shoved the whole lot, fish, bag and everything, up Mr. Wilkins' chimney.

DARBISHIRE: Oh gosh!

JENNINGS: What else could I do? Luckily, it stuck about a couple of feet up and I just had time to nip away from the fireplace before you both came in.

DARBISHIRE: Well, that's all right for now, but we can't leave it there for ever. I mean, think of it in about a month. Mr. Wilkins would have to wear a respirator.

JENNINGS: I know, but I don't quite see how I'm going to get it down. His room's nearly always locked when he isn't there, and even if it wasn't, it's sure to bring down masses of soot and make an awful mess.

DARBISHIRE: Still, something's got to be done; and soon, too.

JENNINGS: I know, I know, don't keep on about it. I wouldn't have done it if there hadn't been an emergency on. But it is a bit tricky, isn't it? I mean, he's only got to sniff to find out there's something spivish peculiar with the atmosphere.

DARBISHIRE: Of course, he might not realise it's coming from the chimney, though; and then, p'raps, he'll start hoiking the floorboards up.

148

JENNINGS: And when he doesn't find it under the floor, he'll call in the what-d'you-call-it, - you know, something like the unhealthy ghost.

DARBISHIRE: Unhealthy ghost?

JENNINGS: Something like that; yes, I know, the insanitary spectre, like Mr. Carter said yesterday.

DARBISHIRE: I think you've got it a bit muddled, but I know who you mean.

JENNINGS: Well, if the spectre finds the chimney full of fish there'll be no end of a hoo-hah; yes, and p'raps you were right about Mr. Carter guessing something, so they'll know who put it there.

DARBISHIRE: It's a dreadful situation, isn't it? My father knows a quotation from Horace about keeping a balanced mind in adversity.

JENNINGS: There'd have been more point if Horace had told him one about how to get fish out of someone's chimney.

DARBISHIRE: I had to learn it, once, er, - *aequam memento rebus...* something or other. Then it goes something like, *in arduis...*

JENNINGS: Oh, shut up, Darbishire! Why d'you always have to start something about what your father says when we're in the most ozard trouble?

DARBISHIRE: 'Cos that's the time when what my father says seems truer than ever.

Slight pause

JENNINGS: I know!... We'll go fishing.

DARBISHIRE: Oh no, we won't. I've had enough to do with fish to last me for a bit.

JENNINGS: Listen; Wilkins' chimney comes out on to the first flat roof and we can get on that quite easily by the fire escape. And we'll take some string and put a hook on the end and go fishing down his chimney and p'raps, if we're lucky, we might be able to hook it up.

DARBISHIRE: H'm... p'raps!

JENNINGS: Well, it's our only chance. We'll try it after cricket this afternoon.

Fade out. Pause. Fade in door knock

MR. WILKINS: Yes?

149

Door opens

Oh, hullo, Carter. Come in.

MR. CARTER: I won't keep you a minute, Wilkins, but I thought you might like to see the winning entry in the camera club competition. There... not bad, is it?

MR. WILKINS: No.   Of course, I don't know anything about photography, but it looks pretty good to me. What is it, - a miner just up from the coal face?

MR. CARTER: No, it's a French fisherman in need of a shave. Still, it's a good photo; it gets first prize.

MR. WILKINS: Good work! Have you got a match on you, Carter. I'm going to light my fire; it's turned a bit chilly.

MR. CARTER: Yes; here you are.

MR. WILKINS: Thanks... Who took that photo, by the way?

Match struck: crackling of burning paper and wood

MR. CARTER: Jennings and Darbishire.

MR. WILKINS: Oh, did they? Judging by the mess they were making in the dark room this morning, I'm surprised anything came out.

MR. CARTER: (*coughing*) I say, does your fire always smoke like this?

MR. WILKINS: No, it's never done this before. Phew! I'll open the window.

Window opened. Wilkins coughs

Pretty bad, isn't it? The room's full of smoke.

MR. CARTER: You don't think there's anything stuck in your chimney, do you?

MR. WILKINS: Shouldn't think so. I'll have a... Good Lord! Look in the fireplace. Am I seeing things?

MR. CARTER: Yes. You're seeing a hook waving about on a piece of string.

MR. WILKINS: What on earth's it doing there?

MR. CARTER: The obvious explanation is that there's someone on the flat roof, letting a piece of string, with a hook on the end, down your chimney.

MR. WILKINS: Yes, but why the...   I'm going to investigate this, Carter. Wait here, till I get back.

Fade to:

DARBISHIRE: Can you get it, Jennings?

JENNINGS: No; I've touched it once or twice, but it keeps dropping down past it, and when I pull it up, nothing happens.

DARBISHIRE: I knew it'd be no good. And you wasted ages putting it down the wrong chimney to start with.

JENNINGS: That must have been Matron's room. Funny if she'd looked in her fireplace and seen my hook waving about.

DARBISHIRE: Wouldn't have been funny if she'd reported us. Anyway, it wasted a lot of time and we can't stay here all day.

JENNINGS: It was wizard interesting, anyhow, finding that old bird's nest in Matron's chimney. I bet she didn't know it was there.

DARBISHIRE: What do birds' nests in Matron's chimney matter? It's this one that's going to bring about our downfall, if we don't get that wretched bag out. Oh, heavens, isn't fish ghastly? I feel I never want to look another one in the face again.

JENNINGS: For once, Darbi, I'm inclined to agree with you. Anyone arranging any fishing competitions, or even serving it up fried, with chips, can include me out of the party. P'raps, in about twenty years, I'd be able to face it, but just at present, anyone who wants fish, can keep it.

DARBISHIRE: Except this lot in Old Wilkie's chimney. Oh, golly, I've just thought of something. S'pose Wilkie lights his fire, - he'll get smoked out.

JENNINGS: We'll have to risk that... It's no good, Darbi, I can't get it.

DARBISHIRE: Oh, help! I can't think what's going to happen now.

JENNINGS: I can... Wilkins is coming up the fire escape. This is the end.

MR. WILKINS: (*approaching*) What on earth are you two boys doing up here? Don't you know it's out of bounds?

JENNINGS: Yes, sir, but you see, sir, we've been doing Matron a good turn, only she doesn't know about it, 'cos she had a bird's nest stuck in her chimney, and we got it out, and if she'd lit her fire, it would have smoked, sir.

MR. WILKINS: Oh, would it! And then, I suppose, you decided to see whether there was a bird's nest in my chimney, too?

JENNINGS: Well, sir, we didn't know about a bird's nest in yours, but we thought there might, p'raps, be something blocking it up.

MR. WILKINS: And you were right; there is.

JENNINGS: Oh! Well, as we'd done Matron's, we thought it'd be a good idea to clear the air in your chimney, just in case it needed it.

DARBISHIRE: Yes, sir, we wanted to spare you any inconvenience. You know, like the poem says, "helping, when we meet them, lame dogs over stiles".

MR. WILKINS: Not a very tactful comparison, Darbishire. Furthermore, this is the second time today I've found you playing the fool out of bounds.

JENNINGS: We haven't been playing the fool, sir; I mean, we certainly didn't come up here for fun. Did we, Darbi?

DARBISHIRE: Fun's about the last thing I should call this racket.

MR. WILKINS: H'm. Both of you will stay in and work on Saturday afternoon.

JENNINGS: Yes, sir.

MR. WILKINS: Now wind up all this string and stuff and report to my room when you've done it and I'll give you your conduct books back.

Fade out. Pause. Fade in:

MR. CARTER: I'm afraid you can't go into your room just yet, Wilkins. You'll have to wait for the air to clear.

MR. WILKINS: Huh! Cor!

MR. CARTER: Did you find anything on the roof?

MR. WILKINS: Did I find anything? I found Jennings and Darbishire. They tried to tell me they were being helpful and taking a bird's nest out of my chimney.

MR. CARTER: Did they actually say there was a nest in your chimney?

MR. WILKINS: They said they'd got one out of Matron's, so I imagined that was what they were after in mine. What else could it have been?

MR. CARTER: I have my own theory about that. You see, while you were up on the roof, the fire perked up a bit, roared up the chimney and whatever was blocking it was consumed by the flames.

MR. WILKINS: Oh, good. Why can't I go in, then?

MR. CARTER: Well, it's left a certain something behind it; a sort of pervading aura. Believe me, Wilkins, it's certainly fresher out here.

MR. WILKINS: Perhaps you're right.

MR. CARTER: I suppose it didn't occur to you why Jennings should have known there was something in your chimney, even before your fire started to smoke?

MR. WILKINS: What? Good Lord! You mean, he put it there, whatever it was? Yes, he must have; he couldn't have known otherwise. Right, I'll have him for that; I'll report him to the Headmaster; I'll see he gets caned.

MR. CARTER: I shouldn't bother. Fate has stepped in and provided a punishment that fits the crime to perfection.

MR. WILKINS: Oh... what?

MR. CARTER: The housekeeper told me this afternoon that the refrigerator at the local butcher's shop has broken down, and we'll be living on fish for breakfast, lunch, tea and supper for the next few days.

MR. WILKINS: That's all right; I like fish. And what's it got to do with a bird's nest in my chimney?

MR. CARTER: Well, if my theory's right, both Jennings and Darbishire will lose their appetite for fish for some time to come.

MR. WILKINS: 'Fraid I don't see the connection. It isn't as though we were feeding them on bird's nest soup.

MR. CARTER: No, but their story sounds a bit fishy to me. Still, perhaps it's just one of those things we shall never know. Speaking of angels, here they are.

JENNINGS: Please, sir, you told us to come for our conduct books.

MR. WILKINS: You'll have to come back later. My room's out of commission.

MR. CARTER: I'm sure you'll both be interested to know that Mr. Wilkins' chimney no longer smokes. Whatever it was that was in it has disappeared completely in the flames.

JENNINGS: Has it, sir? Oh, good, I am so glad. Isn't that
supersonic, sir?

MR. WILKINS: Unusual of you to take such an interest in my comfort.

MR. CARTER: By the way, you two, you'll be glad to know that
you've won first prize in the camera club competition.

DARBISHIRE: Oh, wizzo, super-duper!

JENNINGS: Coo, thank you, sir. What is the prize, sir?

MR. CARTER: It's a book. *The Compleat Angler,* by Izaac Walton.

JENNINGS: Oh! What's it about, sir? Is it exciting?

MR. CARTER: It's all about fish and fishing.

JENNINGS: Oh! It would be, wouldn't it!

Bell rings

MR. CARTER: There's the tea bell. You'd better go and get ready.

JENNINGS: Yes, sir. (*Fading*) I say, Darbi, it's a rotten twizzle
about that book, isn't it.   Never mind, p'raps there's
something super decent for tea; Shepherd's pie or something
really spivish.

Fade out.

JENNINGS
SOUNDS THE ALARM

(Request Week)

Jennings Sounds the Alarm was the seventh Jennings play, written specially for Request Week by popular demand.

It was first broadcast by the BBC Home Service for Children's Hour on 5th April 1949, with the following cast:

JENNINGS	David Page
DARBISHIRE	Loris Somerville
MR. CARTER	Geoffrey Wincott
MR. WILKINS	Wilfred Babbage
HEADMASTER	Lionel Stevens
VENABLES	John Bishop
TEMPLE	David Preston
ATKINSON	John Cavanah
Ld FIREMAN CUPPLING	Frank Atkinson
FIREMAN LONG	Basil Jones
FIREMAN SHORT	Andrew Churchman

Fade in, distant, (recorded) boys singing "Fire Down Below" to
piano accompaniment and hold under.
Fade in Headmaster and Mr. Carter approaching

HEADMASTER: ...and another thing, Carter, so long as I'm Headmaster of this school, I'm determined that the boys shall spend their half-holidays in some useful manner.

MR. CARTER: I quite agree, Headmaster. What do you suggest?

HEADMASTER: We must continually strive to interest them in worthwhile occupations such as hobbies of an instructional nature, or – er – or... Now what exactly is that extraordinary singing noise going on in the music room?

MR. CARTER: That's Wilkins. He's holding a choir practice.

HEADMASTER: Fire practice?

MR. CARTER: No, not fire practice - choir practice.

HEADMASTER: Ah yes, Carter, that reminds me. It's high time we had one.

MR. CARTER: But they're having one now, Headmaster. I just told you; the choir are practising for the concert.

Singing has faded out

HEADMASTER: No, no, Carter. Not choir practice – fire practice. You said so yourself a minute ago. Now when Wilkins has finished making those piano-tuning noises we'll send the boys up to their dormitories and let them come down on the "Penultra Life-Line Escape".

MR. CARTER: Hadn't we better supervise them, Headmaster? They've not used the escape by themselves before.

HEADMASTER: Then it's time they learned to do so. They've only to fasten the strap round their chest and lower themselves gently out of the window. The cable is paid out automatically and the thing's quite foolproof. Yes, it's an excellent instructional pursuit for a half-holiday. In fact, I think we'll go one better and test their initiative thoroughly. We won't *tell* them to come down on the Escape; we'll just say the staircase is impassable and leave it to them to think of coming out by the window...

Buzz and chatter, etc. off

Ah, Wilkins appears to have finished. Let us go in.

Door opens: chatter up/out:

Good afternoon.

OMNES: Good afternoon, sir.

HEADMASTER: Excuse me, Wilkins, I wish to speak to the boys... H'm. Well, now that we've finished with "Fire Down Below" we're going to start on fire up above. Ha-ha-ha... Oh!

Joke not taken

We are going to assume an outbreak of fire on the top landing. Now what is the first thing to do?

DARBISHIRE: Sir! Sir!

HEADMASTER: Yes, Darbishire? I think your hand went up first.

DARBISHIRE: You use your intelligence, sir.

HEADMASTER: Yes?

DARBISHIRE: And if you can't think of anything intelligent, you call one of the masters and do what he says instead, sir.

HEADMASTER: M'yes; quite. But supposing that no master is available? Let us assume that instead of being half past two in the afternoon, it is half past two in the morning, and a boy in dormitory 4 – let us say Jennings, for example – awakens from sleep... (*Slight pause*) I repeat, *Jennings* awakens from sleep!

JENNINGS: (*coming to*) Er – I beg your pardon, sir?

HEADMASTER: The pardon is granted, Jennings. Have you been listening to what I've been saying?

JENNINGS: I – er – I didn't quite catch all of it, no, sir.

HEADMASTER: I said "Jennings awakens from sleep", but judging from your vacant expression, I was beginning to think that you had gone into a state of hibernation for the winter. I trust that is not so?

JENNINGS: I don't know, sir. I don't know what hiber- - what you said, means, sir.

HEADMASTER: It applies to such creatures as toads, moles, bats and, apparently, to some small boys. Derived from the Latin, "hiberna", meaning winter quarters, it means – well, think boy; use your intelligence. What does a bat do in the winter?

JENNINGS: It splits if you don't oil it, sir.

Reaction from boys

HEADMASTER: H'm. Yes. Quite... Well now, let us assume that Jennings discovers a fire and beats the gong as a signal to evacuate the building by the main staircase. But supposing that the stairs have fallen in and he cannot find Mr. Carter. What course of action shall he adopt?

Cries of "Sir! Oh, sir" etc

No, put your hands down; it is for him to decide. He must be guided by the rules for fire drill which are prominently displayed in all dormitories. Well, Jennings, could you cope with such a situation?

JENNINGS: Well, sir, if it's only an *imaginary* fire and we've got to *pretend* the staircase has fallen in, couldn't we imagine that we'd got asbestos suits and pretend... *(to jump out of the window)*

HEADMASTER: Certainly not. Having imagined the circumstances, everything else will be done exactly as though a conflagration had actually occurred. *Exactly*, do you understand?

JENNINGS: Yes, sir, but supposing...

HEADMASTER: There will be no supposing. This is a test of your initiative, Jennings. I shall give you a few minutes to look over the rules and I shall await the result with interest. Now all go quietly up to your dormitories. Come along Mr. Carter and Mr. Wilkins; we'll go outside and wait for them on the quad.

Fade out/in

TEMPLE: Come on, Jennings. You're in charge of this caper. What do we have to do?

JENNINGS: Well, first of all you'd better go and stand by your beds and put your pyjamas on over your clothes.

VENABLES: Why?

JENNINGS: You heard what the Head said. Everything's got to be done as though it's in the middle of the night.

DARBISHIRE: Yes, and when we wake up, the room's full of smoke. I vote we soak our towels in the wash-basin and tie them over our noses.

ATKINSON: Good scheme, Darbi.

JENNINGS: You're crazy! That's not one of the rules. Now, where's that list of fire drill instructions?

VENABLES: It's in the keyhole of the door. I used it to make a bung to keep the draught out. There's a supersonic breeze comes whistling through it if you sleep where I do.

JENNINGS: Well, get it out, then, I've got to read it. I know one thing it says is, we have to close all doors and windows. Something to do with the draught.

ATKINSON: But how can we get out if the doors are closed? And besides, who's going to worry about being in a draught if the place is on fire?

JENNINGS: Well, perhaps it's open all doors and windows, then.

TEMPLE: I think we ought to open all doors to let us out and close all the windows to stop the fire from going out.

DARBISHIRE: But we want the fire to go out don't we?

TEMPLE: Not out of the windows, we don't.

VENABLES: (*approaching*) Here's the instructions; I've got them out, now.

JENNINGS: Bring them over here, then.

VENABLES: Here you are, Jen.

JENNINGS: Now let's see. (*Reading*) Any boy discovering an outbreak of fire at night will sound the gong and inform Mr. Carter who will telephone for the fire brigade. All boys will be...

DARBISHIRE: Yes, but the Head said we'd got to do it *without* Mr. Carter. What's it say about that?

JENNINGS: (*reading*) If no master is available, boys must use... something, I can't read it.

DARBISHIRE: Staircase?

JENNINGS: No, initiative, that's it. (*Reading*) Boys will keep calm and... blah, blah, blah. And then there's a bit at the end that says the dorm prefect will be Wally.

ATKINSON: Who?

JENNINGS: Wally.

TEMPLE: But that's crazy. We haven't got anyone called Wally.

JENNINGS: That's what it says, anyway.

DARBISHIRE: Let me see. (*Reading*) The dormitory prefect will be... Oh, you are a bazooka, Jennings. That's not Wally, that's "wholly". (*Reading*) The dormitory prefect will be wholly concerned with seeing that everyone... (*obeys the instructions*)

JENNINGS: Well, it's time we got cracking. Now you chaps, put your pyjamas on and start opening and closing all the doors and windows and I'll go and biff the gong.

Begin fade.

Dormitory background up and begin fade:

DARBISHIRE: Can I come and be assistant gong-biffer, Jen?

JENNINGS: Okay, Darbi; I'll need someone to hold it steady for me. Come on.

Door opens and shuts

DARBISHIRE: I hope you know what you're doing, Jen. You've got to be jolly careful with fire. My father was making a piece of toast on the gas stove in the kitchen once and suddenly it caught alight and before he knew where he was there was a mighty "swoosh"...

JENNINGS: Why didn't he know where he was?

DARBISHIRE: He did. He was making a piece of toast in the kitchen.

JENNINGS: But you said it went "swoosh" before he knew where he was. And if he was in the kitchen all the time... (*he must have known*)

DARBISHIRE: Oh, don't be such a clodpoll! What about biffing the gong?

JENNINGS: We haven't thought yet how we're going to get down without using the stairs. I'd say that if Mr. Carter's not there to telephone the fire station, I ought to do it myself.

DARBISHIRE: But you can't do that! It's only an imaginary fire. Why not just pretend to phone them?

JENNINGS: Huh! You heard what the Head said when I suggested asbestos suits and pretending to jump out of the window. Everything's got to be done as if this fire's a real one.

DARBISHIRE: Yes, but all the same...

JENNINGS: I shouldn't be surprised if that's what the Head's testing us on, and that's why he told Mr. Carter to keep out of the way to see if we know the proper thing to do. Besides, how else are we going to get out from the top floor if we can't use the stairs? Tell me that; go on, you just tell me!

DARBISHIRE: Yes, of course. P'raps he does mean to phone up then, or why should he have said that?

JENNINGS: The only possible way for us to get out is to send for a fire-escape. I bet you the Head's arranged it. I bet they've got the fire-escape all ready and ticking over waiting for us to give them a tinkle.

DARBISHIRE: Mm – yes – perhaps. Bags you do it, then.

JENNINGS: I shan't let the Head down; he's depending on me, you see. Now first we'll biff the gong, then I'll go round and see that everyone's opening and closing all the doors and windows; then I'll go and look at the stairs and find they've fallen in...

DARBISHIRE: When are you going to ring the fire station?

JENNINGS: That comes last. We've got to do everything in the proper order. I'll go along to Mr. Carter's room, and he won't be there, of course; and then I'll phone up the... (*Doubtfully*) Well, it's bound to be all right, isn't it? At least, I should think so... I mean, at any rate, I hope so.

DARBISHIRE: What are you going to say?

JENNINGS: I'll just say would they mind sending a fire-escape because we're having a bit of a hoo-hah and the staircase has fallen in and there's chaps waiting to be rescued on the top floor.

DARBISHIRE: I still don't think... (*we should be doing this*)

JENNINGS: Oh, shut up, Darbi. Now come on, you hold the gong steady and I'll biff it.

DARBISHIRE: Okay.

Gong sounded. Fade out/in:

LONG: (*singing*) When you walk in the garden...

SHORT: (*singing*) Da-da-da-da...

LONG: (*singing*) In the garden of Eden...

SHORT: (*singing*) Da-da-da-da.

CUPPLING: (*approaching and bursting with energy*) Hey! Break it up! Break it up! This is a fire station, not the Palladium. What are you chaps supposed to be doing?

LONG: Well, as a matter of fact, Archie...

CUPPLING: Not so much of the "Archie". I'm Leading Fireman Cuppling in duty hours, and don't you forget it, Lofty – er, I mean Fireman Long.

LONG: Okay, Leading Fireman Cuppling. Well, me and Shorty here – Fireman Short, I should say – we're doing a bit of brass polishing.

SHORT: Got the standpipe up nice and bright, haven't we?

CUPPLING: It doesn't take two of you to clean one standpipe, does it? And anyway, you're both manning the escape ladder with me this afternoon. It's just been put up on the board, look. (*Reading*) Escape ladder. In charge: Leading Fireman Cuppling. Crew: Fireman Long and Fireman Short. And you're driving, Fireman Long. Now, snap into it, we'll start work right away. It's twenty to three already.

SHORT: Work? What, us?

CUPPLING: Yes, you! Come over here and look at the Escape. Darn my socks, I've never seen such a dirty vehicle! Looks as though it's just come back from a rubbish-dump fire. Tarnished brass, hose badly rolled. We'd better take all the equipment off, and give it a good clean. Come on, get to work. Everything off, now; branches, nozzles, standpipes. Take the hose into the yard and re-roll it. Here you are, I'll chuck it down and you take it outside.

LONG: Tch! Cor! Here, I'm only taking one at a time.

SHORT: Blow me, we ain't 'arf 'aving a spring clean.

Metallic clangs and dull thuds as crew dump the equipment and gag ad. lib. with much gasping and blowing

Where'll I put our boots, Archie? There's so much stuff all over the floor there's no room to put any more down.

CUPPLING: Put them with the other crews' boots – over there by the wall. We'll have them washed before we put them back. Go on, put some beef in it.

More dumping noises

SHORT: Here, Archie, hadn't you better tell the Watch Room as this escape ain't available? Suppose we get a fire call?

CUPPLING: Listen, Shorty. The old fire escape hasn't been sent to a fire for three years, so us having the kit off for ten minutes isn't much of a risk, is it?

LONG: (*coming up*) Well, that's all the stuff off it, thank goodness. Phew! Looks more like a jumble sale in here than a fire station.

CUPPLING: That's better. Now we've stripped everything off we can start cleaning.

Fire alarm bells (electric) go down.
Hold under: running and shouting in background

Fire call! (*Going*) Stand by, you chaps. I'm going to the Watch Room to see what's happening.

LONG: Well, they won't want us, anyway.

SHORT: They better hadn't. Not with our kit strewed knee deep all over the place.

LONG: They'll send No.1 pump, most like. We're all right. It's a rest-cure being on the ladder. It's not been sent to a fire since...

CUPPLING: *(approaching)* Hey, Lofty, Shorty, quick, quick! Escape ladder – it's a turn-out!

SHORT: What, us?

CUPPLING: Yes. Get a move on; I've got the message. Linbury Court School – top floor job – staircase impassable – persons believed trapped – escape ladder needed for rescue.

Alarm bells have stopped

SHORT: But we can't turn out; we've taken all the stuff off.

CUPPLING: Bung it all back on again, then, quick!

They proceed to hurl everything back frantically

Faster! Faster! Chuck it on anywhere for now; we'll sort it out when we get there. But for Pete's sake get a move on.

LONG: Give us a hand with the suction, Shorty.

SHORT: *(panting hard)* That's got it! Cor! This isn't 'arf a carry-on an' all.

CUPPLING: Get the engine started, Lofty, quick. We've wasted over a minute already.

LONG: Okay. Okay.

Self-starter: engine starts sluggishly. Hold under:

She's started. Come on, we've got everything on, now – I hope. Jump on, Short.

SHORT: 'Ere, 'arf a mo'.

CUPPLING: We can't wait any more 'arf mo's.

SHORT: But we ain't got no boots.

CUPPLING: What?

SHORT: You said take 'em all orf, and...

CUPPLING: Quick, they're over there by the wall. Nip over and get them.

SHORT: There's about twenty pairs over here, all mixed up; all the other crews' and I don't know what-all. I can only find one of mine.

CUPPLING: Never mind sorting 'em out. Take the first three pairs and let's get going. Oh! Get a move on, for Pete's sake! Darn my socks, there'll be a row about this!... Ready?

SHORT: *(coming back)* Ah! We'll 'ave to go like this.

CUPPLING: Okay, we're all set, Lofty. Get going.

Engine revs up as appliance moves off with firebell clanging furiously. Fade on this. Fade in:

HEADMASTER: What's all the delay, Carter? Haven't you finished taking that roll call yet?

MR. CARTER: They're all present, Headmaster, except dormitory 4. They haven't started to come down on their Life-Line Escape, yet.

HEADMASTER: Tut, tut.   It must be ten minutes since the gong sounded. What on earth can they be doing?

MR. CARTER: All the other dormitories have been down for some time now. Shall I go and see what's happened to them?

HEADMASTER: Yes, all right, Carter, and tell them in no uncertain terms that I'm most dissatisfied...

Fade to:

MR. CARTER: (*distant, calling*) What are you doing out here on the landing, Jennings? Has anything gone wrong?

JENNINGS: Oh, sir, you can't come up these stairs, sir, because they've fallen in and there's a big imaginary hole where you're standing, sir.

MR. CARTER: (*approaching*) What have you been doing all this time?

JENNINGS: Well, sir, I went to your room like the instructions said, and as you weren't there I did what you would have done if you had been.

MR. CARTER: And what would I have done, had I been there?

JENNINGS: Phoned for the fire brigade, sir.

MR. CARTER: In the case of an actual outbreak, of course, I should... What! Jennings, you don't mean... What exactly have you done?

JENNINGS: Only what the Head said, sir, about using our imagination and all that.

MR. CARTER: Oh, imagination! Thank goodness for that. For a moment I thought you really *had* phoned for the fire brigade. Ha, ha! I was just thinking what would happen if you had.

JENNINGS: But I really have, sir. They ought to be here any minute now.

MR. CARTER: Jennings! You silly little boy! You haven't *really* have you?

JENNINGS: Yes, sir. Haven't I done right, sir?

MR. CARTER: Right? We shall all be prosecuted. False alarm with malicious intent! Oh my goodness, this has put the cat among the pigeons. What on earth possessed you to do a stupid thing like that?

JENNINGS: Well, sir, I thought that was what the Head meant me to do.

MR. CARTER: It didn't occur to you, I suppose, that your dormitory is fitted with a Penultra Life-Line Escape and he was trying to find out whether you'd got enough gumption to use it without being told?

JENNINGS: Oh, goodness, is that what he meant, sir?

MR. CARTER: Naturally! How long ago did you phone?

JENNINGS: Several minutes ago, sir.

MR. CARTER: It's too late to stop them, then. I don't see that there's anything we can do; they'll be here any moment now if they're coming.

HEADMASTER: *(away, calling)* Carter, what is going on? I can't possibly go on waiting any longer. And what are you doing on the landing, Jennings? Go into your dormitory at once.

JENNINGS: Yes, sir.

MR. CARTER: I'm afraid there's been rather an unfortunate misunderstanding, Headmaster. Briefly what's happened is...

HEADMASTER: We haven't time for explanations now, Carter. I'm determined to put that dormitory through its Escape drill and it'll be dark before we've finished at this rate.

MR. CARTER: Yes, but the circumstances... *(are rather exceptional)*

HEADMASTER: Later on, Carter, if you don't mind. I want you to go down and take charge on the quad, and send Wilkins to me, will you?

MR. CARTER: Yes, but Jennings has done something incredibly foolish.

HEADMASTER: He invariably does. I'm going into dormitory 4 and I'll deal with it right away.

MR. CARTER: Yes, but...

HEADMASTER: No, no, Carter, please, another time.

Door opens

What on earth are you boys crawling round the floor on your hands and knees for?

DARBISHIRE: *(thickly)* Please, sir, you said it was the middle of the night.

HEADMASTER: Kindly remove that dripping towel from your face before you answer me. I fail to understand, Darbishire, why you find it necessary to wear a yashmak and pyjamas.

DARBISHIRE: Please, sir, it's because of the smoke and if you keep your nose on the floor you can breathe.

HEADMASTER: Breathe? Smoke?

JENNINGS: It was my fault, sir.

HEADMASTER: I can quite believe it, Jennings. Mr. Carter has already told me that you were responsible for some imbecility, but I never imagined that he meant anything so stupid as this.

JENNINGS: Well, sir, you said pretend it was a real fire and do everything properly and I thought you meant send a message to... Well, sir, what actually happened, you see...

HEADMASTER: I do not see. And I have no time to listen to rambling explanations. When I sent you boys up here, what do you suppose I meant you to use?

DARBISHIRE: Our initiative, sir.

HEADMASTER: Yes, yes, of course; but what else?

JENNINGS: The fire escape, sir. Mr. Carter's just told me. And if they do turn up it won't really be a false alarm because I thought you meant me to send for them, sir.

HEADMASTER: I don't know what you're talking about, boy. The whole lot of you are completely unreliable. (*Turns away*) Oh, there you are, Wilkins.

MR. WILKINS: (*approaching noisily*) Carter tells me you want to see me, Headmaster.

HEADMASTER: I certainly do. These boys have no notion of what is required of them during a fire practice. Will you kindly explain the workings of the Escape to them while I go and inspect the other dormitories.

MR. WILKINS: Certainly, Headmaster.

HEADMASTER: (*going*) And please hurry. The whole thing has been grossly mismanaged.

Dormitory background up

MR. WILKINS: Quiet, everybody quiet. Now come over to the window, you boys, and I'll explain; now the principle on which this – ah – this thing works is extremely simple...

Fade out. Pause. Fade in stalling engine
and fire bell. Hold engine under:

LONG: You don't have to go on clanging the bell out here on an empty road, Archie. Won't make the old bus go any faster.

CUPPLING: I wish something would. Quarter of an hour now since we got the fire call and we've come two and a half miles. Darn my socks, there'll be a row about this.

LONG: It's your own fault, Archie. You should have let us clean the carburettor instead of heaving all that hose about, then we shouldn't be limping along at fifteen miles an hour. She'll never get up this hill, you know. She'll conk out.

Engine chokes

What did I tell yer? She's going to conk out... she's conking...

Engine stops

She's conked. I'll have to have that carburettor off. Take me a
while, an' all.

CUPPLING: Well, get a move on, then; this is awful. We've got
another three miles to go yet and those trapped people on the
top floor – oh my goodness!

Metallic tinkering ad. lib. in the background

Come on, Shorty, get your boots on. There's no point in us sitting
here like a couple of spare puddings while Lofty cleans the
jets.

SHORT: Okay. (*Turns away*) That's funny, I can't find me
right boot nowhere; this boot's a left-footed 'un, so's this,
so's this and so's this 'un. Well, blow me, if I haven't
brought six left boots and no right ones!

CUPPLING: What!

SHORT: It was you rushing me like that at the last minute.
There was about twenty boots, see, all jumbled up and you
said grab the first six, see and...

CUPPLING: All right, all right, don't make a speech about it.
We'll just have to put up with it and wear two left boots...
Darn my socks! Look at the time! (*Turns away*) Get a
move on, Lofty; you don't have to take the whole engine to
bits, do you?

LONG: (*off microphone*) All very well for you to start
moaning, Archie; tricky job these dirty jets are.

Heaving and straining from Short

CUPPLING: Haven't you got those boots on yet, Short?

SHORT: Ooh – ah – wurr! Cor! This right gum boot's two
sizes too small for me left foot. This won't do my chilblain
any good, you know.

CUPPLING: I've got more to worry about than your chilblain.
When I think of that burning building and us stuck here...

LONG: You've said it, Archie. There'll be a row about this. I
wouldn't want to be in your shoes when we get back to the
station.

SHORT: I wouldn't mind whose shoes I was in so long as they
wasn't these 'ere left 'anded gum boots. Cor! They aren't
'arf giving me chilblain the works!

Fade. Pause. Fade in:

MR. WILKINS: Will you listen to me, Jennings, and don't keep staring
out of the window. Anyone would think you were expecting
visitors.

JENNINGS: I'm afraid I am, sir, or rather, I hope I'm not. I mean they couldn't possibly be coming now after all this time, could they?

MR. WILKINS: Stop talking nonsense and listen to me while I'm explaining. Now this metal box thing screwed to the wall is a container. That means that it contains a coil of cable, and protruding through the aperture here...

TEMPLE: What's that mean, sir?

MR. WILKINS: Sticking out of this hole is a strap, or sling, which goes underneath your armpits. And this – er – this gadget here is an adjustable – er – adjuster, which you move up and down if you want to adjust it. In other words, it's adjustable.

VENABLES: What's it just able to do, sir?

MR. WILKINS: I didn't say it was just able to do anything.

VENABLES: Well, what's the good of it, sir, if... (*it doesn't do anything?*)

MR. WILKINS: You sling it along this slide – or rather, you slide it along this sling to tighten the strap across your chest so that you don't – er – slide out of the sling. Now, this second sling and cable must be slung – er – dropped out of the window first, so while you're going down, this other one's coming up ready for the next person, and while he's going down your sling is coming up again.

ATKINSON: But where are you, sir?

MR. WILKINS: Me? I'm here. I'm going to watch you do it.

ATKINSON: No, not you, sir, me, sir – the chap in the sling, sir.

MR. WILKINS: Look here, I'll give you a demonstration and go down first. Now, first I place the sling round my chest like this, and fasten it tight with the adjustable – er – adjuster. Now, I'm all ready to go out of the window.

DARBISHIRE: Hadn't you better open it first, sir?

MR. WILKINS: Eh? Oh yes, of course. Open it, Atkinson.

ATKINSON: (*going*) Yes, sir.

Window opened

MR. WILKINS: Now, I throw the other cable out of the window... so, and I kneel on the window sill like this. Now watch me carefully. I shall get into a kneeling position and push myself gently away from the wall as I go down.

DARBISHIRE: Why, sir?

MR. WILKINS: Why? So that I don't get the sling caught on that ivy that's growing on the wall. Pretty tricky, that ivy, but it's quite all right if you push yourself away from the wall.

VENABLES: But, sir, if you pushed too hard you might get into a tail-spin and...

MR. WILKINS: Be quiet. Now, any questions?

DARBISHIRE: Well, sir, hadn't you better make a famous last speech, sir, just in case?

MR. WILKINS: Don't be ridiculous, Darbishire. (*Going*) Now watch carefully – I'm going now.

Whirr of Escape. Hold:

(*Away*) Now, I want you to observe how I keep my feet stretched out behind...

VENABLES: There he goes. Goodbye, sir.

Stop whirr of escape

TEMPLE: Wow, it's stopped! What's happened?

ATKINSON: He can't be down at the bottom, yet, he hasn't had time.

JENNINGS: Mind out of the way; I'll have a look out of the window. Fossilised fish-hooks!

VENABLES: What's happened, Jen? I can't see.

JENNINGS: Wilkie's got caught on one of those massive branches of ivy just a few feet below the window. (*Calling*) Can't you get free, sir?

MR. WILKINS: (*distant, straining*) Wurr! Corwumph! No, I can't! There's a branch of ivy stuck through the sling, and I can't budge it.

JENNINGS: Quick, Darbi, run and find the Head. He's in one of the other dorms.

DARBISHIRE: Righto. I'll be as quick as I can.

ATKINSON: It's all right. Here he is coming back now.

DARBISHIRE: Goodo. Oh, sir! Sir! Please, sir, it's urgent, sir.

HEADMASTER: You want me, Darbishire?

DARBISHIRE: Yes, sir. There's been a catastroscope, sir. You see, sir, Mr. Wilkins was going down on the Escape quite smoothly, and then suddenly, before we knew where we were...

HEADMASTER: Go on, Darbishire. Before you knew where you were?

DARBISHIRE: Oh, we did know where we were, really, sir. What I mean is Mr. Wilkins is hanging out of the window on the ivy about sixty feet above ground, sir.

HEADMASTER: What? Stand away from that window, you boys... Good heavens! (*Calling*) However did you manage to get the sling caught up like that, Wilkins?

MR. WILKINS: (*distant*) It doesn't matter how; the point is it's got caught and I can't release it.

HEADMASTER: We must do something. Prompt and immediate action. (*Calling*) Wilkins, can't you manage to wriggle free or break the branch, or something?

MR. WILKINS: (*distant*) Wurr! Corwumph! No, I can't shift it. It's firmly wedged through the loop of the sling and I can't get at it to break it.

ATKINSON: Rotten luck, isn't it, sir?

HEADMASTER: Most unfortunate. I shall have all this ivy cut away from the wall first thing tomorrow morning.

MR. WILKINS: (*distant*) What's that you say?

HEADMASTER: (*calling*) I said I shall have the ivy cut down tomorrow.

MR. WILKINS: (*distant*) Tomorrow? But I can't stay here all night!

HEADMASTER: (*calling*) No, no, no; we'll get you up. (*Normal*) Now come along, you boys, we'll all get hold of the cable and pull.

OMNES: Yes, sir.

Gasping and straining

HEADMASTER: Heave!... Heave!... Heave!... It's no good; he's too heavy; we can't move him.

TEMPLE: What about a ladder, sir?

HEADMASTER: We haven't got one long enough to reach so high from the ground. Most unfortunate. We ought to have a really long ladder on the premises. I must order one next time I go to London.

MR. WILKINS: (*distant*) What's that you say?

HEADMASTER: (*calling*) I was saying that I'm going to order a ladder the next time I go to London.

MR. WILKINS: (*distant*) Next time you go to... Corwumph! Have I got to cool my heels out here all that time?

HEADMASTER: Ah, I have it. We must summon the fire brigade and request them to send a long ladder immediately. Now you boys go downstairs while I telephone.

JENNINGS: Please, sir, I've done that already, sir.

HEADMASTER: You've done what?

JENNINGS: I've telephoned for the fire brigade, sir.

HEADMASTER: No!

JENNINGS: Yes, sir. You see I was only trying to use my initiative, and I thought you meant me to...

HEADMASTER: I see. Very intelligent of you, Jennings. I congratulate you on your initiative.

JENNINGS: Well, what actually happened was...

HEADMASTER: That is not to say that boys may normally use the phone without permission, but with Mr. Wilkins in his precarious position, I am inclined to agree that there was no time to be lost.

JENNINGS: Yes, sir.

HEADMASTER: *(calling)* We've sent for the fire brigade, Wilkins.

MR. WILKINS: Thank goodness. How long will they be getting here?

HEADMASTER: *(normal)* Let me see; it's twenty past three and let us say that it's three, or perhaps four minutes since Jennings telephoned and they've got five miles to come, so at the earliest we can't possibly expect them for another...

Fire bell distant: bring up gradually during next speech

Well, I... Bless my... Good heavens, it can't be! Yes, it is! Here they are; they're turning into the drive! Bless my soul, what a remarkable efficient brigade! They must have come at over eighty miles an hour to get here in the time. Downstairs you boys, quickly. I must be on the spot to direct operations.

Fade. Bring fire bell and engine right up, then stop bell and hold engine under, ticking over:

LONG: Well, we're here at last. Thirty minutes it's taken us.

CUPPLING: I can't see anything burning, can you? My goodness, if it's a false alarm after all this!

LONG: Most like it's burnt itself out by this time. What do you think, Shorty?

SHORT: I don't think. My right foot's that uncomfortable stuck in this left 'anded boot, it's gone that numb I *can't* think.

CUPPLING: Switch off, Lofty. There's somebody coming out of the front door. I expect he'll be the Headmaster. He won't half be wild, waiting all this time for us.

Stop engine

HEADMASTER: *(approaching)* Ah, good afternoon.

CUPPLING: Escape ladder, sir; Leading Fireman Cuppling in charge. And I'm very sorry about...

HEADMASTER: Splendid, splendid. You have been quick.

CUPPLING: Eh?

HEADMASTER: One of my assistant masters is – ah – in a state of suspension up there amongst the ivy. Do you see him?

CUPPLING: Yes, sir. Is that all?

HEADMASTER: All? It's enough, isn't it?

CUPPLING: I mean, no fire, or anything like that?

HEADMASTER: No, no fire. Nothing like that.

CUPPLING: Okay. We'll soon get him. (*Shouting*) Get to work, chaps!

Sound of Escape being got into action

TEMPLE: I say, this is lobsterous, isn't it?

VENABLES: Yes. And jolly decent of Old Wilkie to get stuck, specially so's we can see him rescued.

ATKINSON: Look, the fireman's got up to him now.

DARBISHIRE: Yes, he's unhooking him, look, and getting him on to the ladder.

TEMPLE: It's coming down now. Gosh, isn't Old Wilkie lucky! Wish I could come down like that.

DARBISHIRE: He's almost down now... Here he comes!

JENNINGS: (*calling*) Are you all right, sir? Was it nice up there, sir?

MR. WILKINS: I – I – Yes, thank you.

DARBISHIRE: How did you come to get stuck, sir?

ATKINSON: Are you going to do it again, sir, because you didn't really finish your demonstration, did you, sir?

MR. WILKINS: That's enough, Atkinson.

JENNINGS: Sir, perhaps you forgot to gently push yourself gently away from the wall, sir.

MR. WILKINS: All right, all right. Be quiet, all of you. Thanks very much, Leading Fireman. Very smart piece of work.

HEADMASTER: It was indeed. I was most impressed by your speedy arrival.

CUPPLING: What?

HEADMASTER: You must have left the fire station in a flash and streaked along the roads like a rocket.

CUPPLING: Well, darn my socks, I don't get this at all.

HEADMASTER: And I must congratulate your gallant crew on carrying out the rescue with such verve and aplomb.

SHORT: (*aside*) What's that he said, Lofty?

LONG: (*aside*) He said we rescued the bloke with verve and aplomb.

SHORT: (*aside*) No, we never; we used the old Escape.

CUPPLING: We'd better be getting back to the station. They'll be wondering why we've been out so long.

HEADMASTER: So long! Ha, ha, ha! That's very good! Why, with a turn of speed like yours, you must be wearing the winged shoes of Mercury.

SHORT: (*aside*) Well, if these 'ere left 'anded gum boots belong to Mercury he can 'ave 'em back and welcome.

JENNINGS: May I ask the Leading Fireman a question, sir?

172

JENNINGS: Are you all right, sir? Was it nice up there, sir?

HEADMASTER: Certainly, Jennings. What is it? Some mechanical intricacy of the Escape that has set your mind wondering?

JENNINGS: No, sir. I wanted to ask him why all firemen have to have two left feet. Of course, it'd be wizard for playing outside-left, but... (*how would you keep in step for P.T.*)

HEADMASTER: Don't be frivolous, Jennings. Now, had it been some question about the Escape – I'm sure he knows a lot about Escapes, don't you, Leading Fireman?

CUPPLING: Yes, sir. And I think I've just had a very lucky one. Carry on, Lofty. Goodbye, sir.

Chorus of goodbyes. Engine starts and fades to distance

HEADMASTER: Now, before you boys disperse, I wish to say how pleased I am with the commendable behaviour of Jennings this afternoon. I consider his action in telephoning the fire brigade so promptly is an outstanding example of initiative which needs to be rewarded. Don't you agree, Carter?

MR. CARTER: Well, Headmaster, there is another aspect of the matter which I tried to explain to you earlier on.

HEADMASTER: No, no, no, Carter. We must not belittle these examples of initiative which are, alas, all too rare. In fact, I think it would be fitting to excuse the whole school from preparation this evening as a token that I am not slow to recognise meritorious conduct when it occurs.

Clapping and cheers

OMNES: Thank you, sir... Good old Jennings!... Well done, Jennings!... Jolly good!... Wacko!

Fade to music.

WHILE I REMEMBER
the Autobiography
of
ANTHONY BUCKERIDGE

Anthony Buckeridge shot to fame with his radio plays about the fictional schoolboy Jennings, whose adventures in book form have delighted millions of readers around the world. In this autobiography, not only does Buckeridge tell us of the origins of this much-loved character, but he describes a varied and often fascinating life. It begins with his description of the horrific death of his father and moves on through his tough education, his work first in banking and then in teaching, his fascination for the world of theatre, and of course his writing. Buckeridge has produced a heartfelt story which will be as engrossing and entertaining for his countless fans as the fictional exploits of Jennings, Rex Milligan and the Bligh family have been for over 50 years.

David Bathurst, author of *The Jennings Companion*, prefaces the book with a brief sequel to the Companion, and provides an appendix giving some background to the illustrators of the Jennings stories.

Published by David Schutte in softback, A5 size, 96 pages
£8.99 + postage, ISBN 0 9521482 1 8

DS
David Schutte
119 Sussex Road, Petersfield, Hampshire GU31 4LB
Telephone: 01730 269115 Fax: 231177